Key Words in Religious Studies

Ron Geaves

Georgetown University Press / Washington, D.C.

As of January 1, 2007, 13-digit ISBN numbers will replace the current 10-digit system.
Paperback: 978-1-58901-125-0

Georgetown University Press, Washington, D.C.

Library of Congress Cataloging-in-Publication Data

Geaves, Ron.
 Key words in Religious Studies / Ron Geaves.
     p. cm.
 ISBN 1-58901-125-2 (alk. paper)
 1. Religions—Terminology. I. Title.
 BL82.G43 2006
 230.3—dc22

                    2006006886

This book is printed on acid-free paper meeting the requirements of the American National Standard for Permanence in Paper for Printed Library Materials.

13 12 11 10 09 08 07 06   9 8 7 6 5 4 3 2
First printing

Printed in Great Britain

Contents

PREFACE

There were always two intentions behind the conception of the *Key Words* series. The first came to fruition in the glossaries of terminology for each of the five major religions taught in school and university, in response to students who told me that they found the mastering of religious terminology in so many unknown languages and involving unfamiliar concepts to be extremely daunting. The second intention is fulfilled in this book.

The modern student of religion is faced with a vast array of terms from a variety of religions whose specialized vocabulary is often in another language, but the study of religion itself has its own specialized language. Increasingly Religious Studies is a multidisciplinary affair in which technical terms used by the disciplines of sociology, anthropology, psychology, philosophy and theology are becoming common currency, sometimes used in lectures and books with the assumption that the student knows what they mean. All of these disciplines have vocabularies that use certain words and phrases in a precise manner, but sometimes the meaning can subtly change when the same term crosses disciplines and is used by interdisciplinary scholars of religion. It is not possible in a small work such as this to provide a comprehensive glossary of so many disciplinary languages. Each discipline has comprehensive texts concerning its own key words found in either specialist dictionaries or introductions to the field of study. This book attempts only to introduce the generalist student of religion to some of the everyday terminology of Religious Studies. Consequently I have defined Religious Studies very broadly, with no engagement with old debates that differentiate between Theology and Religious Studies. At a pragmatic level, in modular courses, students will find themselves passing twelve weeks on one discipline such as Philosophy of Religion, a similar period on one or more of the world religions, various aspects of Theology and Biblical Studies, as well as a number of methodological or thematic issues. This glossary attempts to reflect this reality and provide a more theoretical companion to the *Key Words* glossaries of individual religions.

So, *Key Words in Religious Studies* enables me to fulfil my second objective. As with the other books in the series, it is limited in size and scope and is bound to reflect the personal interests of the author to some extent. It is only meant to be a resource, a quick reference, to help familiarize the reader with the specialized language pertaining to the theory and methodology of studying religion.

I would like to thank Catherine Barnes, whose patience and support has been remarkable, Janet Joyce who provided the original opportunity for this project to grow from its inception to completion, and Continuum for providing the means for the glossaries to appear in their various editions and for this volume to appear in print.

Absolute   A term used by philosophers and some scholars of religion to depict an ultimate, unconditioned and independent reality or being which need not be a transcendent deity. It has been variously used to describe a self-aware totality of reality, a universal unchanging consciousness or an infinite perfect mind which is expressed in part by individual finite minds. Most systems that posit the existence of an absolute, insist that it is not accessible to the human mind, although glimpses may be perceived. However, some metaphysical systems insist that it is apprehended by the intuition or some capacity of the human that transcends rational thought. (*See also* MYSTICISM; NEO-PLATONISM)

Absolute Dependence   A phrase used by some philosophers and theologians to describe the relationship of creatures to the creator. F. D. Schleiermacher (1768–1834) argued that the feelings associated with absolute dependence provided the key to understanding or interpreting religion.

Acculturation   The assimilation, transformation and possible disappearance of a religious or cultural tradition under the impact of a conquering or dominant civilization or religion. Much contemporary study has focused on the eventual disappearance of religion under the impact of the universal features of modernity moving around the world. Such studies are now seriously challenged. (*See also* ASSIMILATION)

Aesthetics   Traditionally referring to the philosophical study of the beautiful, aesthetics enters the realm of the study of religion through the exploration of the non-literary dimensions of religion such as music, dance, sculpture, painting, architecture and iconography.

Aetiology   A story which offers an explanation of an event, activity or elaboration of a term used elsewhere in the text. For example, the biblical account of the flood explains the origin of the rainbow.

Agnosticism   The suspension or putting aside of acceptance and rejection of religious belief. The modern study of religion often utilizes the idea of 'methodological agnosticism' when exploring religious phenomena. However, sometimes this approach has shifted to the position of critical judgement of a religious belief-system's TRUTH-CLAIMS. Most scholars of religion would consider the latter stance to be methodologically undesirable and fraught with difficulties. (*See also* ATHEISM; THEISM)

Allegory   Many sacred texts contain elements of allegory or can be interpreted as allegorical. In this sense allegory is used as a means of interpreting religious accounts of events as symbolizing or indicating an eternal or metaphysical truth. For example, the story of the release of the Jewish slaves from Egypt and the journey to the Promised Land can be read as an allegory for the liberation of all suffering people by a merciful and just God. (*See also* METAPHOR; MYTH; PARABLE)

Analogy   Usually referring to the process of reasoning from parallel examples, it is one of the recurring features in all religions for DISCOURSE concerning the sacred. However, the MONOTHEISTIC religions are suspicious of the process as it compares the undescribable, infinite creator with the describable finite creation. Analogy is used in the anthropology of religion in the more specialized sense of understanding the logic of MAGIC where in simple terms 'like attracts like'. Magic is perceived to be acts whereby a property is transferred to a recipient object or person on an analogical basis. For example, Evans-Pritchard's study of the Azande notes that when they prick the stalks of bananas with crocodile teeth they repeat: 'Teeth of crocodile are you, I prick bananas with them, may bananas be prolific like crocodile teeth'. Another example of analogy is homeopathic medicine. Analogical thinking is based on resemblances being noticed between natural objects and the belief that the properties of one object can be transferred to another. (*See also* ANTHROPOMORPHISM; MYTH; SYMBOL)

Ancestor Worship   Believed by early anthropologists to be the root of every religion, ancestor worship consists of various practices concerned with appeasing, remembering, revering or honouring ancestors. Typical practices are pouring libations onto graves and offering ancestors food or other gifts for use in the afterlife. There are also rituals for helping the ancestor on his or her way after death by providing gifts for the journey. Ancestor spirits can help their family members but failure to honour them correctly can result in misfortune. (*See also* EUHEMERISM)

Anchorite   A Christian term for a person who withdraws from the world to live a solitary life in a confined space dedicated to prayer, silence and ASCETICISM. The term can be used for the equivalent in other religions but more commonly the term HERMIT is applied.

Androcentrism   The unconscious eradication of women as subjects through the use of male categories to represent the universal. For example, the term 'man' or 'mankind' is frequently used as a universal category to denote humanity. The androcentric perspective would regard the term 'man' as being inclusive of both men and women but without realizing that it is not generic but rather exclusive. (*See also* FEMINISM)

Animatism   An early theory which argued that the first forms of religion must have first conceived of a single power diffused throughout the universe, before it was personified into individual entities. (*See also* ANIMISM; ANTHROPOMORPHISM)

Animism   A belief that the world is populated by individual spirits that live in natural and material objects. Early anthropologists regarded animism as a PRIMAL RELIGION that preceded POLYTHEISM and MONOTHEISM. However, reality is more complex. There are indigenous people who acknowledge a supreme universal creator of the universe, whilst essentially animistic; on the other hand, in strictly monotheistic religions such as Islam, millions of adherents retain animistic beliefs alongside their FAITH in Allah. (*See also* PANENTHEISM; PANTHEISM; PRIMITIVE RELIGIONS)

Anomie A sociological term coined by Emile Durkheim (1858–1917) and literally meaning 'without order', referring to a breakdown or crisis of the moral order within a social group. Anomie, in the study of religion, looks at new forms of religion that emerge from break-downs of individual meaning and order as a result of social disorder. Typical of such manifestations of religion are MILLENARIAN movements, certain kinds of REVIVALISM and FUNDAMENTALISM.

Anonymous Christianity A concept that describes the possibility of salvation for seekers of God who are not church members, have not been baptized into the Christian faith and who through no fault of their own do not know the Gospel message, but never-theless live in a way that attempts to comprehend God's will and to harmonize their lives with it. The concept, best articulated by Karl Raehner (1904–84), opened up the possibility of Christian dialogue with other faiths, removing the difficulties inherent in the idea that all non-Christians were damned. (*See also* ECUMENISM; PLURALISM)

Anthropology of Religion The study of anthropology has traditionally been subdivided into: i) social, that is dealing with human relation-ships; ii) cultural, dealing with what human beings produce or make; iii) psychological, concerned with what they think; and iv) archeo-logical, concerned with human remains. It is quite clear that all of these impact significantly on religion. Historically, sociology and anthropology could be distinguished by a division of subject matter between modern societies and indigenous people. However, today the divisions are considerably blurred. The study of religion, even when not anthropology, is likely to borrow heavily on the methodological techniques developed by anthropologists, especially when the approach to religion is SYNCHRONIC. (*See also* ETHNOGRAPHY)

Anthropomorphism In the domain of religion, anthropomorphism is the attribution of a human personality, qualities or characteristics to a god or divine being. Freud believed that it arose from the lack of knowledge of the world possessed by tribal societies. Anthropomorphism in the sacred texts of MONOTHEISTIC religions becomes a matter of internal dissent regarding whether it should be taken literally or interpreted as symbolic. (*See also* ANIMISM)

Anti-cult Movement A number of organizations and individuals who perceive membership of NEW RELIGIOUS MOVEMENTS in the West to be pathological and requiring escape and desocialization processes in order to free the individual from their psychological grip. Such movements and their leadership are perceived to be exploitative in their relations to recruits, utilizing BRAINWASHING and deception to win new members, depriving them of normal contact with the world to retain membership. Anti-cult movements can be evangelical Christian in origin, consist of disillusioned ex-members, or 'professional' deprogrammers hired by parents to rescue their children who are perceived to have fallen into the hands of the CULT.

Antinomian In Christianity, a term that refers to movements and individuals who argue that grace frees them from the obligation to observe any moral law. The term is used in a wider sense to refer to any religious movements who consider that direct experience undermines the need to observe the moral or ethical codes of the religion. Such groups or individuals can be found in most of the world's major religious traditions. (*See also* ICONOCLASM)

Apocalyptic Originally a term used in Christianity and derived from the visions described in the Book of Revelations that prophesies major disasters consisting of wars, famines, natural catastrophes, and manifestations of the supernatural at the end time. However, the term is now used more generally to describe parallel beliefs in any other religious tradition. (*See also* MILLENARIAN).

Apologetics   Religious writing and scholarship which is undertaken for the purpose of defending a religion against criticism from either opponents or other WORLD-VIEWS. Both Christianity and Islam contain large bodies of apologia.

Apostasy   The deliberate disavowal of belief in the orthodox tenets of a religion. Apostasy can only occur where a religion maintains an exclusive TRUTH-CLAIM, and not surprisingly Islam and Christianity are the two religions with histories of apostasy and punishments for the offence. The history of the Inquisition and the fact of the sin of apostasy being punishable by death in the Qur'an are perhaps the two most notorious examples of reactions to declarations of non-belief. However, Islam has generally held that apostasy is only for those who leave the faith and join another. (*See also* BLASPHEMY; HERESY)

Apotropaic   Literally meaning a 'turning away', it is applied to various kinds of religious phenomena that exist to repel or dispel evil forces. The apotropaic dimension of religious life is concerned with pragmatic elements in everyday life such as health, longevity, fertility, drought, floods and other natural forces that can bring either disaster or prosperity. Furthermore it assumes that these requirements for daily well-being can be controlled by magical means that either enlist the assistance of benign beings or keep away the malign influence of supernatural beings through the intercession of specialist practitioners or ritual activity. The everyday world is assumed to be filled with dangerous spirits and beings from whom protection is essential. (*See also* PRAGMATISM)

Appropriation   Christian theology uses the term appropriation in a very specific sense to signify the DOCTRINE that each of the members of the Trinity are co-involved as a unity in their fundamental activities. For example, all are equally involved in creation but it is appropriate to perceive that God, the Father is the key figure in the act of creation. In a general sense, the term is used to apply to any conscious or unconscious taking-over of a religious idea, doctrine, philosophy or practice from one religion to another.

Archaic Religion   *See* PRIMAL RELIGION.

Asceticism   A variety of practices across several religious traditions associated with a turning-away from the world and a mortification of the senses in order to attain some kind of ideal state of existence either to do with altered consciousness or to appease/draw near to a deity. (*See also* RENUNCIATION)

Assimilation   A term used to describe a government policy towards migrant communities which insists that the newcomers take on the characteristics, values, cultural habits, language and socialization of the majority into which they have settled. Assimilation may create problems where migrant communities maintain religious traditions whose values and practices are different from those of the community entered. (*See also* INTEGRATION)

Atheism   The conscious rejection of a THEISTIC entity creating and controlling human life and natural phenomena. Atheism has emerged as a philosophical alternative with the rise of science challenging the doctrines of Christianity in the nineteenth and twentieth centuries. However, it had already appeared as an alternative DISCOURSE with the weakening of Christianity in Europe during the Enlightenment. Contempoary Islam is also discovering a discourse towards atheism which distinguishes Muslims who no longer practise their religion from those who express disbelief in the central truths of the religion. In some Muslim societies, to be branded an atheist would be dangerous or even a criminal offence if linked to the idea of APOSTASY. (*See also* AGNOSTIC; NON-THEISM)

Atonement   In Christian theology, atonement refers to humanity's reconciliation with God through the sacrificial death of Jesus Christ. However, Jews have a Day of Atonement, an annual festival designed to cleanse people of sin and thus restore good relations with God. Several religions maintain the belief that relations with the divine have been severed and require reunion or restoration. Consequently atonement has been borrowed from its more narrow Christian definition to become a generic term to describe the means by which human beings recover harmonious relations with the divine or the supernatural.

Attributes   More commonly referred to as 'divine attributes', the term indicates the qualities attached to God in the sacred texts of the respective religions. The MONOTHEISTIC religions of Christianity, Islam and Judaism developed sophisticated philosophical and theological debates concerning the existence of God's attributes and their relationship to His oneness, especially the possibility that unity may be undermined. There was also the fear of ANTHROPOMOR-PHISM diluting the concept of 'otherness' and leading human beings into the danger of comparing God with the creation. In spite of these reservations, the names of God's attributes have become practices of contemplation and prayer, as in, for example, the 99 names of God mentioned in the Qur'an as attributes of Allah.

Authenticity   Ways in which religions affirm that their TRUTH-CLAIMS are genuine or real contacts with the sacred. Recourse to REVELATION, experience, SACRED TEXTS, religious founders, tradition, religious authority enshrined in institutions, moral and legal codes, and religious functionaries can all be drawn upon to provide authenticity to religious NARRATIVES.

Authority   Used to describe issues of control and power in a religious tradition. Control may imply leadership over a religious organi-zation or over the articulation of correct doctrines and practices. Authority may not necessarily be invested in human beings but in SACRED TEXTS, objects, REVELATION, tradition or religious experi-ences. However, such sources of authority are manipulated and interpreted by human sources. Some may be the official interpreters of an institutionalized religion, whilst others may claim that their personal experiences override the official sources of authority. When this occurs, the discord can lead to persecution and schism. (*See also* AUTHENTICITY; HERESY; INSTITUTIONALIZATION; LEGITIMATION)

Autonomy   A term used to describe the condition of life as independent of any external authority in moral or ethical decisions. The same principle is applied to knowledge, which is regarded as being only the product of human reason. One powerful strand in the study of religion asserts that all religious knowledge derives from human experience and reason and is not the product of REVELATION or other manifestations of the divine. (*See also* RELIGIONIST)

Avatar *See* INCARNATION.

Behaviourism   A method in psychology that ignores all data derived from introspection or other mental states in favour of a rigorously defended 'scientific' paradigm that argues that all knowledge of the mind must be discovered through observation in laboratory conditions. Behaviourists understand the human self as reducible to biophysical and neurological responses to stimuli. Such modes of thought can still be found in recent work on altered states of consciousness experienced by religious practitioners. (*See also* REDUCTIONISM)

Being   A metaphysical or philosophical term for that which is ultimately real or has existence. The opposite of being is non-being or nothing, but there is an intermediate stage of 'becoming', usually interpreted by metaphysical systems to indicate the possibility of apprehension of being through moving from imperfection to perfection, incompleteness to completeness, fragmentation to wholeness. (*See also* ABSOLUTE; MYSTICISM; NEO-PLATONISM)

Belief Systems   Religions are sometimes referred to as 'belief systems', but the label is problematic as some religions, such as Buddhism, consider their doctrines to be established on experience rather than belief. In everyday language, 'belief' is used to describe an utterance for which evidence of its truth or validity is suspect or unproved. However, religious believers claim that their respective FAITHS are expressions of TRUTH-CLAIMS that are given ultimate or absolute value. (*See also* FAITH TRADITIONS; TRADITIONS)

Biblical Criticism   A phrase embracing a wide application, but inclusive of all modern attempts to neutrally apply the methods of textual criticism and analysis used in other disciplines to the texts of the Bible. Because such research into the Bible or any other religious text is identical to the task applied to any secular text, that is an attempt to reconstruct literary and historical realities, tensions can develop between researchers and those who maintain the text to be sacred and sacrosanct. (*See also* COGNITIVE DISSONANCE; FORM CRITICISM; REDACTION CRITICISM; STRUCTURALISM; TEXTUALISM)

Biblical Studies   The academic study of the Bible utilizing literary criticism, HERMENEUTICS, linguistics, archaeological discoveries and any other means to discover meaning in the text. Although still functioning in some centres of Christian learning as a tool for reinforcing or clarifying FAITH, modern scholarship of the Bible treats the text in the same way as any other piece of literature under investigation.

Biblical Theology   Any theology which bases itself on Scripture; however, it refers specifically to the reaction to liberal theology led by Karl Barth (1886–1968), in which the sufficiency of the Bible was asserted as the source of all theological knowledge, thus emphasizing the uniqueness of biblical concepts over and above the influence of surrounding cultures.

Bioethics   A body of ethical debates arising out of various issues in biology – for example, genetic engineering, environmental issues, cloning of animals. In many of these conversations, religion plays a role, as it has traditionally provided the ethical and moral guidelines for human behaviour, especially concerning the value or sanctity of life. (*See also* ETHICS)

Blasphemy   Language regarded as being insulting or derogatory towards a deity or the sacred. During the history of Christianity, the concept of blasphemy was developed beyond abuse of the deity to include heterodox belief or HERESY. Blasphemy in certain periods of history has carried the sentence of death and remains part of the legal statutes of the USA and the UK, although its meaning has once again transformed to become public offence to religious sensibilities. Islamic law retains the original meaning of insulting language towards God but minority Muslim politics has begun to campaign for blasphemy laws to be extended towards Islam in order to protect Muslims from statements in the media or from the public which offend against their religious sensibilities.

Body Theology   A phrase which connotes a variant of theology that deals with questions concerned with personal and social attitudes towards the body, in particular recognition and respect for gender minorities, medical ethics, holistic medical care, nourishment and protection of the environment, and FEMINIST THEOLOGY. All these take their roots in the idea of the body being a creation of God, to be respected and cared for. Such theologies tend to be integrative rather than dualistic with regard to the relations between body and spirit. (*See also* ENVIRONMENTALISM; QUEER THEOLOGY)

Boundaries   A term used to describe the borders placed by social, cultural and religious groups to mark who is in and who is out. All religious movements and traditions operate with boundaries which are to a lesser or greater degree permeable but all have membership rules. The study of boundaries is significant to develop knowledge of IDENTITY construction. (*See also* EXCLUSIVIST; INCLUSIVIST; MARGINALITY)

Brainwashing   The idea that NEW RELIGIOUS MOVEMENTS (NRMs) or cults were able to use extreme forms of mind control to recruit and to keep followers dependent became part of the DISCOURSE of ANTI-CULT MOVEMENTS, penetrated the media and to an extent entered the study of psychology during the 1970s. A number of articles and books have been written across various disciplines central to the study of religion, debunking the theory of brainwashing. They usually take two forms: i) if cultic membership was able to override the brain's normal capacity to process information, then tests on members should demonstrate pathological symptoms; ii) if NRMs or cults possessed such extraordinary powers to brainwash recruits to the degree that the individual's free will was negated, then how was it that most attendees at introductory meetings and seminars avoided conversion? In addition, most studies indicate a very high drop-out rate from all new religious movements.

Bricolage   A term used by the anthropologist Claude Lévi-Strauss (b. 1908), in his discussion of myth. It refers to a *bricoleur*, a craftsman who uses whatever is available or on hand to complete a particular task. It has been widely adopted to refer to the construction of symbolic structures from a wide variety of culturally available symbols.

Canon An authoritative body of sacred texts deemed to contain the orthodox and accepted doctrines of a religion or a tradition within a religion – for example, the Pali Canon of Theravada Buddhism. The canonical texts of Christianity are those included in the authorized versions of the New and Old Testaments. The historical process by which a canon comes to be accepted is often negotiated over several centuries as part of the INSTITUTIONALIZATION process that takes place after the death of a founder. In Buddhism and Christianity, for example, the creation of the definitive canons took place through the decisions of a number of councils. (*See also* SACRED TEXTS)

Cargo Cults Religious movements of the Melanesian islands in the South Pacific which developed from the belief in magical access to the white man's goods that were landed by sea and believed to have been stolen from the tribal ancestors. Such religious movements are MILLENARIAN to the extent that they believe in a future time when the indigenous people will live in peace and harmony in a new social order.

Casuistry The philosophical activity of bringing general moral or ethical principles to bear on individual cases.

Celibacy The life-long practice of abstinence from marriage or any other sexual relations. Various religious traditions have different attitudes towards celibacy, ranging from obligatory requirement, respect, encouragement, to condemnation. For example, Islam condemns celibacy but, in practice, where observed by ascetic Sufis, it was given respect by the populace. Christianity adopted celibacy for its monastic orders and priesthood, probably from the fourth century. Buddhism and Jainism embraced it as an ideal, creating elite monastic or ascetic lifestyles. (*See also* ASCETICISM, CONTINENCE)

Charisma In Max Weber's (1864–1920) famous definition, 'a certain quality of an individual personality by virtue of which he is set apart from ordinary men and treated as endowed with supernatural, superhuman, or at least specifically exceptional powers or qualities. These are not accessible to the ordinary person, but are regarded as of divine origin or as exemplary, and on the basis of them the individual concerned is treated as a leader'. Others have built on Weber's work and attempted to classify various types of charismatic authority that exist amongst religious traditions. The most significant use of the concept of charisma is applied in the examination of religions from their origins to the development of traditions. In this kind of cyclical analysis it is argued that religions begin with a charismatic leader and then become routinized and INSTITUTIONALIZED after the founder's death. However, this traditionalism is not perceived by some followers to match the insights and depth of experience of the original founder and his followers. New groups emerge that break away in an attempt to revive the original spirit. (*See also* EXPERIENCE)

Chastity *See* CONTINENCE.

Christocentrism The view that outside of the REVELATION of Christ there is no salvation or redemptive knowledge of God. (*See also* ANONYMOUS CHRISTIANITY; ECUMENISM; EXCLUSIVIST; INCLUSIVIST)

Christology The study of the nature of Christ with particular emphasis on the relations between the divine and human aspects of his being. Historically such perspectives have ranged between Christ as fully human through to completely divine, with the dominant or ORTHODOX position being fully human and fully divine. The various positions taken up that differ from the orthodox DOCTRINE have been a major source of HERESY where either Christ's divinity or humanity have been denied.

Church   A term denoting both a religious building and a community within Christianity. 'Church' is often used to represent the total community of the saved within Christianity. In classic sociological theory, church, as opposed to sect or denomination, represents the totality of all Christians. Sometimes those writing about other religions will use terminology such as the 'Buddhist church' or the 'Sikh church'. Such terminology is best avoided, as other religions have their own specialized terminology to describe collectivities or buildings and they rarely imitate Christian forms of organization.

Circumstantialist   *See* SITUATIONALISM.

Civil Religion   A phrase first coined by Rousseau in his book *The Social Contract* (1762), referring to religion which reflects the values and the virtues of the state. This may range from state religions to quasi-religious rituals and language codes used by the state to express and reinforce such values. Generally, the phrase refers to religion that cannot be separated from the state and is essential to the state's survival and stability over a period of time. So, civil religion may consist of celebratory occasions, memorial rituals, NARRATIVES of exemplary persons or events in history through which the state impresses itself emotionally on the minds of its citizens.

Classification   There have been many attempts to arrange religions or religious phenomena in classes or categories but most are unsuccessful, as they often contain implicit biases or assume an evolutionary model for the development of religions. For example, attempts to classify often assert that MONOTHEISM is somehow the pinnacle of religious evolution. Although attempts to find classes or categories of religious life can be useful in grouping material for analysis, the student needs to be aware that the process of classification itself may require analysis. (*See also* EVOLUTIONIST)

Cognitive Approaches   Cognitive approaches to the study of religion focus upon the findings of cognitive science and psychology to infer how religious ideas are acquired, maintained and transmitted through the everyday workings of the mind. Such theorizing focuses on explaining religion rather than interpretation of beliefs and practices. (*See also* COUNTER-INTUITIVE; INTUITIVE ONTOLOGY; PSYCHOLOGY OF RELIGION)

Cognitive Dissonance   A psychological theory of consistency that can be applied to religion to explain how individuals or groups manage the existence of dissonance or inconsistency between treasured beliefs and actual events. The theory of cognitive dissonance was developed by Leon Festinger (1919–89), who argued that dissonance or inconsistency was uncomfortable and that individuals would attempt to decrease its impact on their psychological lives. Therefore cognitive dissonance can be perceived as a reactive condition which leads to activity orientated towards reduction of dissonance, frustration, disequilibrium. Dissonance can be caused by new information or events that do not fit the previously held WORLD-VIEW or contradictions between beliefs and everyday actions. Classic examples of cognitive dissonance in religion would be the failure of prophesy, unexpected behaviour on the part of a religious leader, new knowledge that impacts on the truths of a religion, or tragic events that undermine belief.

Collective Representations   A way of perceiving the world that is held in common by members of a social group or a religious movement. These are transmitted from one generation to another and therefore presume that continuation is a function of birth rather than individuality. (*See also* COSMOLOGY; METANARRATIVES)

Colonialism   Colonialism can be defined as the military or political domination of one nation over others in order to achieve economic benefits. Colonialism impacts on the study of religion at the level of questioning the production of knowledge within the context of power relations and how conquered or dominated populations are represented by those in authority. Seminal to such thinking were the works of Edward Said (1935–2003) on ORIENTALISM and critics of post-colonialism from previously colonized nations who have developed SUBALTERN theories. In addition, the interaction between colonizers and the colonized creates new forms of religion either as reactions or as part of a process of hybridization. (*See also* HYBRIDITY)

Communalism   A term usually used in the context of India to describe the process evident in the nineteenth and twentieth centuries whereby Indian religions became markers of political identity and 'otherness'. Increasingly, Indian Muslims, Hindus and Sikhs have organized themselves into the key political factions within the context of power DISCOURSE and action, often leading to a variety of religio-political identities considered as forms of FUNDAMENTALISM, asserting superiority and separation.

Communitas   A sense of emotional belonging arising from shared egalitarian, spontaneous and inclusive relationships, which was believed by some anthropologists to be the significant function of religious life-cycle rituals and PILGRIMAGES. It was argued that certain religious ceremonies and occasions moved the participant out of the normal hierarchical roles imposed by society into a shared inclusive experience of community outside of the structures of everyday life. Communitas was seen to be at the heart of pilgrimage but this has been challenged by studies that demonstrate that social roles are not always suspended on such occasions.

Comparative Religion   A sub-discipline of the study of religion that developed from the idea that it was necessary to compare material from different religions and across different periods of human history in order to establish a 'scientific' study based on an impartial and systematic method. It was in vogue from 1870 to the beginning of the twentieth century. Unfortunately the attempt to discover a typology based on comparison never achieved its aim of impartiality, and often made judgements on the relative superiority or inferiority of religions in relation to each other, usually privileging Christianity. The original intention of comparative religion, that is to observe the religions of the world as phenomena rather than beliefs to be followed or practices to be observed, is now found under the title of Religious Studies or the Study of Religion in Britain or the History of Religions in Europe. (*See also* EVOLUTIONISTS)

Confessional Approach   The confessional approach to the study of religion is where adherents of the religion communicate ideas in order to convince or promote the TRUTH-CLAIMS of their religion to outsiders or to further confirm or elucidate the faith to other believers. Such an approach generates its own type of scholarship but is distinct from the approach of social sciences or the humanities, where religion is studied as a human activity to be understood. (*See also* APOLOGETICS; EMIC)

Conscience   The human capacity to live in conformity with such principles considered to be for the moral good and acceptable, and the faculty which acts as a guide or monitor that such behavioural codes are being adhered to. Individual conscience is in a sense distrusted or regarded as imperfect by most of the world's major religions, and they require in some way that conscience be based upon divinely-given ethical codes. This is most forcefully articulated in the MONOTHEISTIC religions of Semitic roots, which consider that REVELATION is required to provide conscience with clear guidelines of divine origin.

Consecration   The public ritual act of providing sanctification and blessing to a person, building, land or material object so that it becomes part of a sacred domain. For example, buildings that are becoming temples, churches or other sacred sites are formally consecrated in most major religions.

Constructivism   A position taken towards ETHNICITY which sees it as both i) determined and ascribed through birth and socialization processes drawing upon NARRATIVES of the group's ancient and sacred past; and ii) transformable and shaped in response to changing circumstances. (*See also* PRIMORDIALISM; SITUATIONALISM)

Contemplation   Contemplation in a Christian sense refers to an act or condition of simple loving focus upon God and his gifts. Defined by St John of the Cross (1542–91) as 'the soul must be lovingly intent upon God, as a man who opens his eyes with loving attention'. In Christianity, contemplation is contrasted with MEDITATION, which is more specifically used to describe discursive prayer, often upon a text to elicit deeper understanding. (*See also* MYSTICISM; PIETISM)

Continence   Restraint from sexual intercourse for a period of designated time and practised for a specific religious reason – for example, periods of fasting, retreat, particular sacred festivals or periods of the year marked by abstinence. (*See also* CELIBACY)

Contingency   A philosophical concept that refers to an event or a being that could not have occurred or existed without some other event or being first occurring or existing. The cosmological argument for the existence of God states that everything cannot be contingent but that eventually a being or event must be arrived at which had no predecessor but was ultimately causal. (*See also* COSMOLOGICAL ARGUMENT)

Continuity   The belief held by religious adherents that their religion is an unchanging and absolute entity created by God or some other form of sacred entity. Such beliefs consider that all tradition, acts of worship, SACRED TEXTS, and codes of conduct appear complete in the origin of the tradition, which in itself may be considered to be outside history.

Conversion   The kind of changes involved in the decision of an individual or a group of people to change their allegiance from one religious tradition to another, either as a result of missionary activity or to gain advantage in social, political or economic status. Conversion can also refer to movement from one group within a religion to another within the same religion, or from non-involvement in religion to allegiance to any one particular religious tradition. Sometimes conversion can also be used to describe a particularly intense amplification or intensification of religious feeling or allegiance, especially where nominal or apathetic affiliation is replaced by the experience of the religion becoming central to the life of the individual concerned. (*See also* REVERSION)

Cosmology   The way in which a group of people, community or culture views the world and its formation, thus creating broadly similar systems of practice and belief. Understanding cosmologies can provide the scholar of religion with a larger picture with which comprehension of specific details can be shown to make sense to the adherent. However, it is essential to remember that the student or researcher gazes out from the cosmological view of their own culture. (*See also* ETHNOCENTRISM)

Cosmological Argument   Philosophical arguments for the existence of God which begin by stating that everything that is moved is moved by something else and that logically we must arrive at a prime mover or first cause. Other types of cosmological arguments refer to sufficient reasons for existence. (*See also* ONTOLOGICAL ARGUMENT)

Counter-intuitive   A theoretical construct for analysing religion developed by Peter Boyer (1998). He argues that the human mind is not made up of random associations but rather combinations of ontological categories such as persons, animate beings, artifacts, events and abstractions, each containing domain-specific expectations. Boyer argues that once people have developed such ontological categories, violations can occur that run against the expectations and forms of natural behaviour of members of individual categories. For example, gods or ghosts have properties that violate the category of physicalness. These violations are named counter-intuitive as they contradict human INTUITIVE ONTOLOGY.

Creed   A formula which encapsulates the essential doctrines of a religious tradition and which is considered to contain the necessary beliefs one requires in order to be seen as an orthodox believer. Creeds are negotiated over time and represent the victory of a particular faction within highly contested political and religious struggles. Christianity is the only religion with fully developed creedal statements, although Islam, Sikhism and Judaism have passages taken from their SACRED TEXTS which can be used in the same fashion. As ORTHODOX statements, creeds can also be used to ascertain who is inside or outside the fold of correct adherence to the religion. Non-conformity to DOCTRINES contained within creeds can lead to penalties. (*See also* HERESY)

Cult   A complex of religious activity directed towards a common object of reverence (be it deity, saint, animal, spirit or, indeed, a living human being), that is the members of the cult are united by the fact that they all worship the same object, rather than the fact that they all hold the same views or dogmas. You 'belong' to a cult only as long as you care to practise it, and membership is seldom exclusive; it is generally possible to participate in more than one cult at a time. However, this classic anthropological use of 'cult' has been undermined by usage of the term by the popular media and the ANTI-CULT MOVEMENTS who use it in a much more pejorative sense to describe NEW RELIGIOUS MOVEMENTS which they believe to possess highly restrictive borders; place followers under the control of irrational or exploitative leaders, BRAINWASH in order to keep recruits, and practise deception on their followers.

Culture   Most cultural interpretations of religion are immanentist, that is they account for religion as confined to its historical or cultural location and interpret religion as a factor in human existence rather than a system of ultimate value. The most striking feature of most cultural approaches to religion is RELATIVISM, both in regard to religious knowledge which is perceived to be historically or culturally constructed, and in positing relativity amongst the NARRATIVES of the religions themselves. Both relativities are difficult for the religions. (*See also* IMMANENTIST)

Deconstructionism A critical method associated with POSTMODERNISM that asserts that the identity of the author is irrelevant to the interpretation of the text. The idea of seeking for 'true' meaning is made redundant as no interpretation can hold more authority than another. Thus deconstructionists tend to read a text through the process of dismantling perceived or given 'meanings'. Deconstructionism is most significant in reassessing dominant interpretations of SACRED TEXTS.

Deism A system of natural religion that holds to the view that God is the creator of the world, even accepting the idea of a life after death, but generally rejects REVELATION or the belief that God maintains an interest in the world. Belief in divine rewards and punishments is usually abandoned.

Demythologization Associated with the Christian theologian, Rudolf Bultmann (1884–1976), who argued that Christianity had to come to terms with the challenge of modern criticisms of its TRUTH-CLAIMS by exploring the mythic and symbolic language of the Bible and then restating it without the mythological which, he argued, is located within a particular cultural/historical WORLD-VIEW. The descriptions of the world taken for granted by the Biblical writers are ignored, eliminated or reinterpreted so that the message becomes pertinent to contemporary readers. Similar processes are occurring to varying degrees in the interpretation of the SACRED TEXTS of other religions but the challenge for demythologizers is how to reformulate the religion in a new and authentic way without losing something essential. (*See also* MYTH)

Deontology   A term used in ethics to describe a position in which the moral agent is motivated by the requirement to act from duty or obligation.

Determinism   The belief that whatsoever takes place is determined by prior causes or conditions, and so it appears that the future is already fixed. In many religions forms of determinism exist, either based on the idea of PREDESTINATION, divine omniscience, theories of karma or fate. There are a variety of positions within each such tradition concerning the role of free will or human agency. (*See also* OCCASIONALISM)

Dharmic   One aspect of a fourfold CLASSIFICATION system derived for the analysis of Indian religions. Dharma is concerned with religious organizations or structures that are based on a divinely ordained prescribed set of rules that govern the universe and human behaviour. The Hindu caste system would be an example of a dharmic category; 'dharmic' describes religious practices that are performed to either maintain or obey prescribed sets of rules believed to be divinely ordained and are a common feature of Indian religions. (*See also* KISMETIC; PANTHIC; QAUMIC)

Diachronic   The process of studying a religion through examining its historical development, from origin through to contemporary formations. Traditionally this approach has focused on the study of elite groups, famous people, significant events and their causes. (*See also* SYNCHRONIC)

Diaspora   A term first coined to describe the communities of Jews living in exile in various parts of the world and separated from their homeland in Israel. Increasingly the term has come to be utilized generically to describe the experiences of political or economic migrant communities. In the study of religion, the focus is on religious diasporas – for example, Muslim, Sikh or Hindu communities outside of their places of origin. (*See also* ETHNICITY)

Dimensional Approach   A model for exploring religion that avoids definition in favour of identifying the basic features of a religion. There are various attempts to identify the dimensions of a religion but arguably the best known and most influential has been that proposed by Ninian Smart (1927–2001). His dimensions were: the doctrinal/philosophical; the narrative/mythic; the ethical/legal; the ritual/practical; the social/organizational; and the experiential/emotional. There is no hierarchical notion of significance regarding each dimension, although examination of a religious tradition may reveal that one dimension is more prominent than another. Dimensions are a useful tool for description, allowing the vast array of data available to be organized. (*See also* ETHICS; EXPERIENCE; DOCTRINE; MYTH; NARRATIVE; PHENOMENOLOGY OF RELIGION; RITUAL)

Discourse   Discourse theory posits that religions are no more than socially constructed realities in which a system of relations are given meaning by the participants. Discourse need not refer to language or texts; it is used to describe any system of interrelated meanings such as behaviour, clothing, architecture or religious ritual, where messages are conveyed by symbolic coded behaviour which embodies or acts out a discourse. (*See also* POSTMODERNISM)

Divine Attributes   *See* ATTRIBUTES.

Doctrine   The body of religious beliefs and tenets that is taught or passed on with AUTHORITY and which constitutes a religion's COSMOLOGY or WORLD-VIEW. (*See also* HERESY; ORTHODOX)

Dualism   A term which is used in a variety of ways in the contemporary study of religion to signify the existence of two independent principles. In classic Christian THEOLOGY it was usually used to describe metaphysical systems that maintained that good and EVIL are the creation of two equal and separate powers or to describe the DOCTRINE that Christ had both a human and a divine personality. Other forms of dualism typically found in religions are the division between body and spirit, matter and mind. (*See also* MONISM)

Ecclesiology   Used in two ways to describe either the study of churches as edifices – for example, their buildings and interior architecture, or the study of the theology of the Church as an organization.

Eclecticism   A kind of syncretism where new forms of religion are created by picking and mixing from a variety of existing religious traditions. Eclectic mixing is likely to create forms of religion whose borders are less fixed. (*See also* HYBRIDITY; SYNCRETISM)

Eco-feminism   A form of FEMINISM that struggles for fair and equal distribution of the earth's resources rather than exploitation of nature. Nature itself is perceived as sacred and the Earth is regarded as divine and feminine, embodied in the notion of GAIA, the ideal that the planet is a living unified organism. The old MONOTHEISTIC religions are seen to be hopelessly patriarchal and exploitive and eco-feminists seek a global religion that is rooted in ecology and affirms the sacredness of the female. Eco-feminism will often revive ancient forms of goddess worship. (*See also* ECO-RELIGION)

Eco-religion   Contemporary religious movements which stress the sacredness of the earth itself and the dependence of human beings upon the survival of the planet. Such religions usually affirm nature as sacred in itself and critically view the MONOTHEISTIC religions as based on exploitation rather than harmony with nature. There is much more sympathy with indigenous religions which are perceived as embodying connectedness with the life force. (*See also* ECO-FEMINISM; INDIGENOUS RELIGION)

Ecstasy   The joyful sense of being lifted out of oneself and transported into the immediate experience of the deity or some sacred realm. Generally ecstasy is described as a transient and intense state of rapture. Ecstasy can be associated with the condition of the mystic and the prophet or any other form of religious rapture where the self is temporarily lost. (*See also* MYSTICISM)

Ecumenism   A movement within Christianity to draw together the various factions or denominations into a visible whole, either in dialogue and cooperation or in actual union with each other. Ecumenism can also operate at the level of worship, where Christians either worship in each other's churches or devise new forms of worship that bring together different denominational factions. On occasions, the term ecumenism can be found used in the context of similar efforts by other religions.

Eidetic Vision   The ability to see what is actually there. Related to the phenomenological approach to the study of religion, eidetic vision presupposes the ability of the researcher to see objectively into the essence of a religious phenomenon. (*See also* EMPATHY; EPOCHE; PHENOMENOLOGY OF RELIGION)

Emanation   A way of thinking about the world and God which perceives the creation as being a ray or an outflow from the absolute being of God rather than the product of a divine workman. (*See also* GNOSTICISM; NEO-PLATONISM; PANTHEISM; PLATONISM)

Embodiment   The study of the human body as performative and embodying categories of identity through physical idioms, such as food practices or decoration, that come to represent cosmological understandings of the universe.

Emic   The emic perspective results from studying behaviour as from inside the system. In the study of religion, this is equated with the insider's viewpoint. However, it is important to realize that the emic perspective not only belongs to the religious insider of any respective religious tradition but also pertains to academic writing which attempts to produce as faithfully as possible the informant's own descriptions of practices and beliefs. (*See also* ETIC)

Empathy   Not to be confused with sympathy, empathy is a state of mind achieved by the researcher whereby he or she attempts to 'feel in', to understand what is inside another individual or group. In the well-known dictum of Ninian Smart (1927–2001), empathy can be described as 'moccasin walking'. Smart stated that empathy needed to be structured, that is, the researcher is required to build a detailed picture of the WORLD-VIEW of the religious adherent. (*See also* DIMENSIONAL APPROACH; EPOCHE; PHENOMENOLOGY OF RELIGION)

Empiricism   The idea, associated with the production of knowledge, according to which things are knowable because they are apprehended by the experience of the senses. At a crude level, religious believers, especially Christians, who build their COSMOLOGY upon FAITH, have found themselves under criticism by empiricists. However, other religions, for example, Buddhism, assert their own forms of empiricism, in which they argue that their claims are verified by EXPERIENCE.

Enchantment   Originating in Max Weber's (1864–1920) theorizing on rationalization, where he argued that the rationality of advanced industrial societies destroyed the 'magic garden' or 'enchanted garden' of the pre-modern WORLD-VIEW where the sacred was perceived to be existent and commonplace in the everyday world. Enchantment is used to describe processes whereby the sacred world is protected, reinstated or revived or maintained against the secular. For example, the contemporary phenomenon of New Age is regarded as a form of re-enchantment. (*See also* MODERNITY; SECULARIZATION)

Endogamy   The practice of certain religious and caste groupings to maintain closed borders by not allowing marriage outside of the group's members. The Indian caste structures are probably the most well-known example of endogamy but the religions of Judaism and Islam have forms of modified endogamy pertaining to restrictions on women from marrying outside the tradition.

Environmentalism   If environmentalism can be defined as movements to protect the planet and its life-forms from overzealous and uncontrolled human exploitation of natural resources, then the question has to be asked what role the religions of the world can play in such activity. Thus the topic of religion and environmentalism seeks to discover and foster religiously derived ethics, COSMOLOGIES and practices that can be used to support ecological concerns. In addition to ethics, some religions maintain WORLD-VIEWS that see the world as interrelated and interdependent parts of an organic whole, often imbued with a single life force or seen as a living being. (*See also* ECO-RELIGION)

Epiphany   Derived from the Greek *epiphaneia*, meaning 'manifestation', the term is usually associated with the Christian holiday with the same name held on 6 January. However, it has a wider meaning where it can describe any manifestation of a divine or superhuman being. (*See also* EXPERIENCE; MYSTICISM; THEOPHANY)

Epistemology   A branch of philosophy concerned with what we know and how we know it – in other words, knowledge and how it is acquired. An important question of epistemology related to the study of religion is how belief differs from knowledge. Scholars of religion also have to ask what presuppositions and beliefs they are holding and which inform the questions they ask in order to acquire knowledge of a religious tradition.

Epoche   Sometimes referred to as 'bracketing', it is applied to the attitude of the researcher where judgement of the beliefs and practices about the other under investigation is suspended or bracketed out in order to avoid describing them from one's own point of view or belief system. (*See also* EMPATHY; PHENOMENOLOGY OF RELIGION)

Eschatology   Originally used to describe the study of the final destiny of the human soul and the eventual fate of humankind in Christian systematic theology, the term has been broadened to include all such religious COSMOLOGIES arising from other traditions that deal with the final fate of either individuals, communities or humanity.

Esotericism   A term used to describe religious movements which claim that there is an inner secret meaning to the religious tradition they emerge from, known only to the initiate or the possessor of a spiritual knowledge not conferred on all the believers. The secret knowledge is claimed to be passed down by the initiated throughout time, often dating back to the original REVELATION. In this way esoteric movements see themselves to have a more authentic or higher understanding of the religion than that maintained by ordinary adherents. Esoteric groups may claim that they have an inner interpretation of the SACRED TEXT or an inner knowledge of the SACRED. (*See also* AUTHENTICITY; EXPERIENCE; THEOSOPHY)

Essentialism   An essentialist position within the context of the study of religions is usually taken to be located in the work of a number of significant figures with their roots in liberal Protestantism – for example, John Hick (b. 1922), Ninian Smart (1927–2001) and Wilfred Cantwell Smith (1916–2000), who have adopted a pluralist position based on the idea of an existing 'essence' that unites all the world's major FAITH TRADITIONS, despite the evidence of diversity. Feuerbach (1841) argued that each religion contained an essence and that early phenomenologists provided a methodology for identifying and classifying essences in particular religions. In such essentialist approaches, religion is presented as a series of separated traditions, each containing its own discrete and distinctive beliefs and practices, and each with nothing in common with the other. (*See also* NOMINALISM; UNIVERSALISM)

Eternity   A common feature of THEISTIC religions is the contrast made between the mutability or changing nature of creation subject to transitory birth, existence, decay and death and the immutability or unchanging, timeless nature of the supreme being or creator-God.

Ethics   A branch of philosophical study that is concerned with questions of values by which societies live, such as justice, duty, love and virtue. With regard to the study of religion, ethics explores the rules and principles which form part of religious ways of life. In today's complex societies, ethics needs also to observe the interrelations between religious moral systems and medical ethics, political ethics and business ethics. (*See also* BIOETHICS; PHILOSOPHY OF RELIGION)

Ethnicity   A group IDENTITY which is constructed and maintained by people who perceive themselves as sharing in common a unity based on several factors which can include language, common history, dress codes, food, music, a shared sense of homeland, customs and religion. Ethnicity is usually studied as an aspect of migration and identity. (*See also* CONSTRUCTIVISM; PRIMORDIALISM; SITUATIONALISM)

Ethnocentric   The perspective from within a cultural or religious group that brands outsiders as somehow less than human or lacking all of the requirements to be judged as real or full humans. The work of the anthropologist Lévi-Strauss (b. 1908) demonstrated that ethnocentrism was inherent within human collective life. In addition, ethnocentricity is used to define the sense of superiority that privileges the narrative of the scholar over and above that of the cultural or religious group under observation. (*See also* EUROCENTRIC; ORIENTALISM)

Ethnography   Ethnography is sometimes used as an alternative term for fieldwork. 'Ethno' relates to 'people' and 'graphy' to 'picture', thus it describes research where the researcher is present in person to gather the data and thus provide a 'people picture'. Ethnography can refer to the process of fieldwork or the final product. The field researcher is in the position of a stranger who gradually acquires the knowledge of the insider but in the process achieves objectivity not always available to the true insider. They are interested in direct experience of the world and some ethnographers even argue that researchers should try to surrender themselves to the culture under observation. However, whatever the approach to fieldwork, it challenges misconceptions that can arise from too much reliance on textual research. It is fluid and does not involve extensive pre-fieldwork design. One can change in mid-flow, follow leads that arise in the field, but remain flexible and observant. (*See also* ANTHROPOLOGY OF RELIGION; PARTICIPANT OBSERVATION)

Etic   A viewpoint that studies behaviour as from outside a particular system. In the study of religion the etic perspective is the outsider's attempt to collect material, categorize, organize, compare and interpret religious beliefs and practices in terms of his/her own frame of reference, usually drawn from the theories of social sciences or other academic disciplines. (*See also* EMIC)

Euhemerism   Named after the Sicilian writer Euhemerus (c. 315 BCE), the term was adopted to describe an evolutionary theory which believed that the ghosts of remote ancestors or famous predecessors eventually acquired the status of gods. (*See also* ANCESTOR WORSHIP)

Eurocentric   A perspective of the world that privileges European thought and culture over and above all others. Closely associated with ORIENTALISM, Eurocentrism in the study of religion can be found at the level of a scholar writing on other religions and cultures from the standpoint that secular humanist post-Christian democracies are superior forms of civilization, or at a more sophisticated level, there is the question posed by some post-colonial SUBALTERN theorists that the academic production of knowledge itself is Eurocentric.

Evil   Most religious COSMOLOGIES contain NARRATIVES and DISCOURSE to explain the existence of both human propensity to bad or harmful actions, thoughts or speech and natural misfortune. For THEISTIC religions the major questions are the origin of evil and how its presence can be compatible with the existence of an omnipresent and good deity. There are a variety of explanations of a philosophical, theological and metaphysical nature, ranging from religion to religion. They may be crudely subdivided between those who attribute evil to another agency in competition with God and those who argue that evil arises from ignorance.

Evolutionists   Scholars of religion influenced by Darwin, especially in the nineteenth century, who created categories of religion based on hierarchical formations arranged in an order in which their own civilizations and religions were at the top, Asian civilizations and religions were in the middle and so-called 'primitive' societies were at the bottom. All societies and civilizations were deemed to be in an evolutionary process in which they would advance from simple and primitive to complex and rational. Religions were also categorized and placed on this evolutionary ladder with ANIMISM and TOTEMISM near the bottom and MONOTHEISM at the top. (*See also* COLONIALISM)

Exchange Activity   A tool for the analysis of religion borrowing from the language of economics. Exchange activity sees religion in terms of construction and production of meaning. Drawing upon Spiro's (1970) definition of religion as 'culturally patterned interaction with culturally postulated superhuman beings', those who perceive religion as exchange activity study the relations of exchange between followers of a religion and their respective deities and the relations of exchange between various groups within the religion. (*See also* SPIRITUAL CAPITAL)

Exclusivist   A term used to describe a religion or group within a religion who believe that their claim to possess the sole truth regarding doctrines and practices expressing the true nature of divinity and its relation to the human, ultimately negates all other TRUTH-CLAIMS put forward by rival religions or WORLD-VIEWS. (*See also* INCLUSIVIST)

Exegesis   The process of explaining a SACRED TEXT in order to penetrate further into the author's meaning or to apply new interpretations based upon contemporary situations or enhanced knowledge. (*See also* HERMENEUTICS)

Existentialism   A variety of philosophical, theological and religious positions which are marked by the emphasis on the individual as opposed to the communal or traditional; the role of active individual participation in the quest for meaning and truth; and the performance of life decisions rather than acquiescence or conformity to prevailing social or religious systems. Philosophically the existentialists begin with concrete or real human situations rather than speculative theories or BELIEF SYSTEMS concerning abstract or universal truth. Some contemporary scholars of religion chart the shift from INSTITUTIONALIZED religion towards personal spirituality in the context of a shift towards individuality and existentialism. (*See also* POSTMODERNISM; SPIRITUALITY)

Exogamy   A religious or cultural custom which insists that a man marries outside his own tribe or community.

Exorcism   Practices performed by a religious specialist which are believed to cleanse the human being or a location from possession by EVIL spirits, ghosts, djinn or various kinds of otherworldly beings thought to cause harm. Certain illnesses may be perceived to be caused by malevolent spirits and to require exorcism in order to effect a cure. Exorcists may be specialists drawn from outside the ORTHODOX ranks, such as shamanic figures or the low-caste *ohjas* of village Hinduism; on the other hand, they may be performed by official representatives of the divine such as Christian priests or Muslim *imam*s, who have received formal training in such practices. (*See also* EVIL; KISMETIC; SHAMAN)

Experience   Religious experiences could arguably be described as the essence of SACRED life from which all the other dimensions of religion originate. Such experiences range across the spectrum of human feelings, including awe, love, peace, ecstasy, contentment, intense longing, fear, and sensations of oneness, unity or possession. In many religious traditions, feelings of oneness, possession, submission or loss of ego-self are regarded as the pinnacle of experience and in some religions systematic disciplines have been developed to assist in bringing about such experiences. The possibility of religious experiences divides those scholars who consider such experiences of the sacred to be unique and different from all other realms of human experience and those who maintain there is nothing that separates such experiences from any other domain of human existence. (*See also* MYSTICISM; NUMINOUS; TRANCE; SHAMAN)

Faith Although often used as an alternative to 'belief', the term is more problematic when used in the study of religions, for two reasons. The first is the very specific meaning given to faith in Christianity where it refers to both the body of truth which fully incorporates the teaching of Christ and to the human response to the REVELATION of such a body of truth. In the latter sense, faith is a supernatural or grace-given state and is dependent on God's working on the human soul. The second difficulty arises in some Eastern religions – for example, Buddhism and certain aspects of Hinduism – which consider themselves to be empirical, in the sense that if certain disciplines are followed, then definite experiences will follow as a result. Therefore, faith has to be understood within the context of each religion and the label of FAITH TRADITIONS commonly used to describe religious communities may not sit easily with some.

Faith Traditions A phrase sometimes used as an alternative to 'religions'. Although no longer of current usage in the study of religions, it can still be found as common currency in interfaith bodies. The difficulty with the term stems from the very specific definition of FAITH as applied to Christianity, where it is used to describe an activity of God. In the Middle Ages, faith was perceived to be a higher form of knowledge than REASON and a distinction was drawn between truths accessible to the human intellect and those knowable only by an act of God. The application of the term as an umbrella to describe religions fails to recognize that some religions have no place for faith at all, but rather regard their doctrines to be based on empirical evidence arising from EXPERIENCE. Others do not consider belief to be significant and focus on praxis. (*See also* BELIEF SYSTEMS; TRADITIONS)

Fallibilism   The view that a system of beliefs is always open to correction and revision as no set of doctrines can be certain. Fallibilism sits in contrast to the philosophical position of FOUNDATIONALISM.

Feminism   Feminism in the study of religion has lagged behind other academic disciplines and has not been given the weight that it deserves. However, women working in the field have not only challenged interpretation of SACRED TEXTS at the level of offering new understandings, but have also questioned the production of such texts as a male activity. In addition, new feminist theology has been developed by Christian women. Female activists have also challenged the role of men in positions of authority and the lack of female roles in RITUAL. They have also examined the use of masculine-specific language in PRAYER, liturgy and sacred texts. Muslim female writers have attempted to recover the voices of women in history and to ascertain the relationship between Islam and cultural patriarchy. (*See also* ANDROCENTRISM; GENDER; PATRIARCHY)

Flagellant   Individuals who inflict minor injuries on themselves either by beating their bodies with various objects – for example, chains, whips, thorns – or by body piercing. The reasons for these kind of activities vary from religion to religion depending on the respective MYTHS and DOCTRINES. For example, Christian flagellation may be to imitate the sufferings of Christ or as an act of penitence. The famous processions at the festival of Muharram where male Shi'ite Muslims beat themselves with chains is done in order to share in the suffering of the MARTYR, Hussain, Muhammad's grandson.

Fideism   A term applied to a number of religious traditions which argue the incapacity of the intellect to achieve knowledge of the divine and instead emphasize FAITH. However, this is a largely a position of the MONOTHEISTIC religions with their belief in

REVELATION. In Eastern religions, a variation of fideism emphasizes religious EXPERIENCE over and above rationality and REASON.

Folk Religion   *See* APOTROPAIC.

Form Criticism   A translation of the German *formegesschichte*, it refers to a method used first to research the Gospels and then other New Testament books. The basic methodology involves attempts to uncover an earlier oral tradition behind the written texts. (*See also* REDACTION CRITICISM)

Foundationalism   A term used in the PHILOSOPHY OF RELIGION to describe a type of textual interpretation which bases its analysis on the concept that there is a fundamental truth in the text which cannot be challenged. Consequently any interpretation is constructed upon the foundation of the text's truth value and cannot contradict it. Foundationalism forms the most common type of analysis carried out by adherents of the faith and is central to the textual literalism maintained by fundamentalist groups. (*See also* FUNDAMENTALISM; TEXTUALISM)

Free Will Defence   A philosophical position arising from debates on the nature of evil which posits that evil is not the responsibility of God as it originates from the human capacity to make choices. Classic THEISTIC free-will theory argues that God necessarily had to give human beings choice to make decisions with regard to moral actions, and this provided the possibility of making wrong or evil choices. Such arguments sit in contrast to DETERMINISM. (*See also* PREDESTINATION).

Functionalism   A sociological and anthropological term used to describe a methodology and a perspective which explores various components or subsystems of a social system and examines their functionality within the whole. Most famously associated with Durkheim, Malinowski and Radcliffe-Brown, functional approaches to religion perceive it to be useful to the good functioning of the total system, especially with regard to religious values and practices creating a kind of social cement to ensure stability. Similar approaches can be found in the PSYCHOLOGY OF RELIGION, but with the emphasis on the functioning of the individual. (*See also* REDUCTIONISM; STRUCTURALISM)

Functionalist Definitions   Definitions that refer to the phenomena of religion in the context of what they can contribute to the well-being of the individual or the social system. In describing religion as functional to a particular social system, culture or psychological state, the particular beliefs and practices associated with the religion become insignificant in themselves. (*See also* REDUCTIONISM; SUBSTANTIVIST DEFINITIONS)

Fundamentalism   Any contemporary religious movement with a coherent IDEOLOGY which seeks to bring religion back to the centre stage of public life as well as private life. There may be shared characteristics such as: resistance to secularization; antagonism or critique of other religious forms, including those in their own traditions which are seen to have compromised with modernity; an activist stance towards establishing their religion at the centre of public life as well as private life; claimed authority over a scriptural tradition of the religion; application of technology whilst rejecting MODERNISM. Various forms of fundamentalism can be found in most of the world's major religions.

G

Gaia The view that the planet Earth is a living, self-sustaining organism capable of maintaining itself in stability and harmony. Thus the entire range of living beings and organic matter is regarded as constituting a single living entity. The Gaia hypothesis was put forward by James Lovelock (b. 1919), an atmospheric biologist, who took the name from the ancient Greek goddess of the Earth. Gaia has not only become an important concept to ENVIRONMENTALISM but also to ECO-RELIGIONS and some FEMINIST movements who take the idea back to its roots and resurrect the idea of the original earth-goddess.

Gender A term used to shift debates away from stereotypical understandings of sex difference as determined by nature/natural forces to a more complex understanding that such differences are a category of human experience influenced by social relations. (*See also* ANDROCENTRISM; FEMINISM; PATRIARCHY)

Globalization Globalization is simply defined as a process in which both space and time are becoming increasingly compressed as communication technology advances. Globalization literature focuses on two aspects: i) space/time convergence; ii) cultural homogenization, with particular focus on the increasing domination of Western values and consumerism. However, the construction of a globalized space has resulted in the creation of new locations and forms of religion created through community consciousness and self-conscious constructions of ethnic identity. Consequently globalization brings into play religious forces that can operate to both connect and differentiate the world. (*See also* HYBRIDITY; INDIGENEITY)

Gnosticism   A complex of pre-Christian Mediterranean religious movements that were to develop unique forms within early Christianity. Although Christian Gnosticism eventually declined or developed into separate sectarian movements by the end of the second century CE, it remained as an influence on Western ESOTERIC movements and some of its mythology has re-emerged in popular form in novels, most notably Dan Brown's *The Da Vinci Code*. Gnosticism was distinguished by its focus on the idea of *gnosis*, a revealed knowledge of God and the origins of creation and purpose of humankind. It is through the revelation of such knowledge that the spiritual dimension of the human being can be saved. Borrowing from NEO-PLATONISM, Gnosticism posits a emanationist view of God, in which the unknowable absolute becomes first the demiurge or creator-God, and finally manifests as matter. Gnosticism is usually dualistic, in that the world is perceived as a battle between cosmic forces of good and EVIL. In order to return to the state of God's purity, the human being needs to be freed from the tyranny of matter and return to the spiritual essence. Christian Gnosticism held that the apostles had received a special secret knowledge from Jesus which they could pass on to initiates, although sometimes, the secret knowledge could be received direct by REVELATION to the leaders of their various sects.

God   A term which is used in two senses, first the general, in which it is applied to all religions which possess a worshipped supernatural entity that in some way can control the destinies of human beings and therefore needs to be appeased. However, it takes on a more specific meaning in the MONOTHEISTIC religions where there can only be one such being who is also the creator of the universe, standing in a relationship to the creation of both TRANSCENDENCE and IMMANENCE. There are so many diverse understandings of the nature and being of God, not only across religions but also within a single world tradition, that many scholars of religion prefer to utilize terms like 'sacred', 'supramundane' or 'supernatural' to refer to the domain of God/gods. (*See also* POLYTHEISM)

Grace   Usually associated with Christianity, where it refers to a divine intervention of God into human life in order to aid or facilitate the return to sanctity. Essentially the theology inherent in the doctrines of grace arises from the impossibility of human effort to approach the sacred. In Christian terms this arises from the fallen nature of humankind. The idea of grace occurs in some forms of Hindu THEISM and forms of Chinese and Japanese Buddhism which venerate the Amida/Amitabha Buddha.

Great Traditions   A term used in contrast to LITTLE TRADITIONS and coined for particular application to Indian religions. It refers to all-India forms of Sanskrit literature and culture whose deities, rituals and SACRED TEXTS are universally acknowledged and claimed to be ORTHODOX by certain religious elites. Of interest to the scholar of religion is how such traditions come to be constructed and the inter-relationship which they have with local traditions.

Hagiography   The body of literature on the lives of saints and holy men and women. Hagiography is especially concerned with insider accounts of MIRACLES and legends, but has developed to assess and compare the sources, ascertain the historical significance of the person, and provide a more critical account of the significance of legendary accounts of miracles. (*See also* HAGIOLOGY)

Hagiology   Texts whose subject matter is the lives and legends of holy men and women and the religious activity that develops from their inspiration. (*See also* HAGIOGRAPHY)

Hegemony   Simply referring to power relations or ruling elites, hegemony impacts on the study of religion in the fields of GENDER, religious stratification, colonialism, language, and, from a Marxist perspective, the relationship of dominant religions and political power structures.

Henotheism   A term coined by Max Muller (1823–1900) to describe religions that believe in many gods but regard them all as aspects of one supreme being. In such types of religion, typical of Hinduism, individuals or groups may focus their attention on any one of the range of deities available as the sole or supreme manifestation of the ultimate reality. (*See also* MONISM; MONOTHEISM; POLYTHEISM)

Heortology   The study of church festivals within the ecclesiastical year and their origins, history and meaning.

Herberg Thesis   The theory that the religious consciousness of ethnic or migrant populations is stronger than that of other mainstream communities because religion offers a strong identity during times of dislocation. The theory is named after Will Herberg (1901–77), an American sociologist who studied immigrants in the USA. (*See also* ETHNICITY)

Heresy   The assertion by members of a religious community that they hold to certain beliefs or practices that differ substantially from those established as ORTHODOX and given authority by the majority of the group. Usually heresy is given public recognition and incurs penalties when asserted by the leadership of religious movements. (*See also* AUTHORITY)

Hermeneutics   Usually used to refer to the theory of the interpretation of texts. The subject area of hermeneutics in religion is SACRED TEXTS and their original meaning, developing to incorporate their meaning for contemporary readers. The latter provides a new significance to the subject in that it begins to address the question of how it is possible to understand the DISCOURSES of the past from the view of the present. Such discussions have led to the expansion of hermeneutics into literary criticism, social philosophy, aesthetics and social sciences. (*See also* EXEGESIS; HERMENEUTICS OF SUSPICION)

Hermeneutics of Suspicion   A phrase coined by Paul Ricoeur (1913–2005) to describe the approach to textual analysis that is rooted in a belief that the 'truths' or NARRATIVES of a SACRED TEXT were undermined by modern criticism. Texts that were perceived to contain the story of the world's reality supplemented by divine AUTHORITY were now perceived distorters of reality, a false consciousness to be identified before true humanity could be reclaimed. Ricoeur describes Freud, Marx and Nietzsche as the 'masters of suspicion'. (*See also* HERMENEUTICS)

Hermit   An individual who chooses to live alone, renouncing both the world and communities of fellow renunciates. In Christianity, hermits usually belong to monastic communities and require the consent of such communities to live the solitary religious life. In other religious traditions it is not usually so structured. However, hermits require some kind of support system and offer scholars of religion the opportunity to explore the social networks of an apparently individual activity.

Heterodox A term meaning 'not ORTHODOX'; however, the problem for the study of religion is in determining whose view should be regarded as orthodox. Most religions are marked by heterodoxy and claims to orthodoxy are disputed. Religions such as Islam and Hinduism have no prevailing central body to define orthodoxy and the process whereby one viewpoint arises out of a number of heterodoxies to successfully position itself as orthodoxy is in itself a political and historical process and may not necessarily indicate the mainstream viewpoint.

Heuristic A philosophical term for any hypothesis that is used to provide guidance or inspiration in the process of discovery. 'Heuristic' can be applied to a number of standard methods used in the scientific study of religion – for example, the MODEL and the PARADIGM. (*See also* IDEAL TYPES)

Hierarchy Most religions have a hierarchical or socially ordered structure based on value or power, in spite of a possible rhetoric of equality. Where religions have become linked to state, the status of their functionaries is usually linked to power. However, other religions may base their social order either on perceived relationships to the deity or on the ability to attain particular states of consciousness linked to the end goals of the tradition. For example, Theravada Buddhists and some Jain movements acknowledge a fourfold hierarchy of male monks, female monks, male laity, female laity. Other religions base both religious and social hierarchies on a divine or cosmic principle of order.

Hierophany *Lit. 'a showing of the holy'*. A term used by Mircea Eliade (1907–86) to define moments or incidents in history when the divine manifests some aspect of itself to someone. He makes two subdivisions of hierophany: (i) KRATOPHANY, the showing of sacred power; and (ii) THEOPHANY, the showing of a god. In its widest sense, hierophany is any kind of phenomenon that reveals or manifests the sacred. Hierophanies may be overt in the sense that they are linked directly to MYTHS, SYMBOLS or customs and easily understood, or they be may be hidden within a code that needs to be deciphered.

Historical Criticism A method of rediscovering the past as presented in SACRED TEXTS of the world's religions, employing the methods of historians. The basic premise of historical criticism is that there can be no direct access to events of the past other than data, and no datum can be beyond suspicion. Eye-witness accounts, for example, can be partial and even distorted. Consequently historical criticism approaches all such data within sacred literature with scepticism. In order to achieve this, various methodologies are utilized in order to yield all available information from the data. (*See also* HERMENEUTICS OF SUSPICION)

Historicism The theory that social, cultural and religious phenomena are determined by history and which perceives historical development as the most basic aspect of human existence.

Historiography The study of history writing and the construction of history.

Holism An approach to the study of religion, common to both sociology and anthropology, that sees religious phenomena as part of larger cultural or social wholes rather than demarcating a uniquely 'religious' field of experience separate from the non-religious domains of existence. (*See also* ANTHROPOLOGY OF RELIGION; SOCIOLOGY OF RELIGION)

Holy *See* SACRED.

Homilectics The art of preaching as taught to Christian ministers and concerned with the sources of sermons, their content, progression, structure and delivery. There is also the possibility of homilectics being applied to Islam and the Friday sermon delivered by the imam. Muslim education for imams would offer students training in sermon delivery and content, but very little academic study has taken place on this process.

Humanism   A term which includes any philosophy or teaching that emphasizes the dignity and value of human life, looks to the welfare of all human beings and takes pride in human achievement. Modern humanism, at least since the Enlightenment, has been marked by anti-religious sentiments, and attempts to create an alternative WORLD-VIEW where the virtues and ethics extolled by religions are perceived as purely human values and do not require recourse to a divine entity such as God. Humanists can be ATHEIST or AGNOSTIC, and the latter may find it easier to work with religious adherents on issues of common ground such as the quest for peace and justice.

Hybridity   Sometimes referred to as hybridization, the term refers to a group of scholars who focus on contacts, relations and exchanges in the colonial and POST-COLONIAL environment. In contrast to INDIGENEITY perspectives, such theorists explore SYNCRETISM, cultural and religious exchanges both in the relations between colonial powers and the colonized, and in the development of post-colonial migrant communities.

Hylozoism   The DOCTRINE that all matter contains life. Although typically associated with indigenous religious traditions, it is also common amongst Indian traditions and most fully developed in Jainism where it informs a vigorous application of non-violence to all beings. (*See also* ANIMISM; PANTHEISM)

Iconoclasm   In Christian terms, iconoclasm refers to a variety of movements that have been opposed to the use of images as focuses for devotion and worship. In a less specific sense, iconoclasm is used to describe those who attack cherished beliefs and practices. In other religious traditions, iconoclasm can describe those who have attacked the external practices of the religion – for example, RITUALS, ceremonies, PILGRIMAGES and legal codes – in favour of direct experience of the SACRED. (*See also* ANTINOMIAN)

Iconography   The ways in which a religion represents the divine or the SACRED in visual forms such as statues, paintings and bas reliefs. (*See also* ICONOCLASM; IMAGERY)

Ideal Types   A sociological tool for comparison. Ideal types are models of categorization that do not exist in reality but are established for the purposes of analytical comparison by collating characteristics from concrete actual phenomena which are more or less present. A classic example of an ideal type would be the church/sect typology. (*See also* METHODOLOGY)

Idealism   In the broadest philosophical and theological sense, idealism is contrasted with MATERIALISM and refers to those who position themselves on the side of consciousness, REASON or mind as opposed to matter as the reality of the existence.

Identity   Theologically identity is concerned with the significance or reality of the person, especially continuity of the self after death. However, the term is used sociologically or anthropologically in terms of an individual's location of selfhood within the parameters established by participation with a group and the group's subsequent location of itself within the wider society. The movements of religions around the world through the processes of MIGRATION, and the impact of GLOBALIZATION upon local communities have brought the issue of identity to the forefront of the study of religion.

Ideology   It is possible to find some scholars who define religion as ideology or complete ways of life and patterns of thought organized to produce meaning or significance for human action. However, religions go wider than this in that they are also COSMOLOGIES and MYTHOLOGIES. Ideology is usually taken to imply a political course of action, and some religions are distinctly non-political. It should be noted that many politically active Islamicists refer to Islam as an ideology that is superior to capitalism, socialism or Western forms of democracy. (*See also* WORLD-VIEW)

Idolatry   The worshipping of idols or images of deities believed to be false or unreal gods. The concept of idolatry is central to the MONOTHEISTIC religions where it becomes a major sin. In some forms of contemporary Islamic DISCOURSE the sin of idolatry has been extended to include admiration or allegiance to human-created systems of governance that are seen to replace God's sovereignty, such as democracy, socialism, and SECULARISM.

Imagery   The representation or imitation of something by something else. Religions, by definition, are full of images, as the worlds of the SACRED with which they are concerned to communicate are beyond the material or mundane life. The term 'image' is used in the study of religion to avoid the contentious term 'idol' when describing attempts to convey divinity in animal or human forms. (*See also* METAPHOR; SYMBOLS)

Imagined Communities   A term used in anthropology and originally applied to the analysis of nation and identity but now beginning to be used for religious communities and the formation of identity. The term 'imagined' does not mean that the beliefs and practices are in some way false. It is imagined because the members of the community will rarely know all other members, meet them or even know their identity but they will hold in their minds an image of fellowship around a set of common identity markers, in the case of religion maintained by common beliefs and practices. Thus common identity is assumed where it may not actually exist. All communities above a very small size are 'imagined'.

Immanence   The idea of God's omnipresence in the universe and the subsequent extension to the indwelling presence of the SACRED within the human person. In the MONOTHEISTIC traditions, God is usually perceived as both immanent and TRANSCENDENT, although groups of adherents focus on one or the other, creating different religious moods. In simplistic dichotomies, the transcendent is said to lead to feelings of the NUMINOUS, where the immanent is more likely to lead to mystical traditions. (*See also* MYSTICISM)

Immanentism   The position of an individual or group that stresses the divinity's indwelling presence in the world, or, alternatively, a philosophical position that argues that all events or phenomena can be explained in terms of other events in the world and excludes the possibility of divine intervention. (*See also* IMMANENCE)

Immutability   A theological term to describe the DOCTRINE that God or divine nature does not undergo change in its mode of being.

Impassability   A theological term used to describe the inability of God or divine nature to experience pain or suffering. Both arise out of the allied concepts of God's timelessness and IMMUTABILITY.

Incarnation   The belief that divinity can manifest in human or animal forms usually for the salvation of other beings or the benefit of the world. The most well-known incarnation belief is the Christian DOCTRINE that Jesus Christ was both fully God and fully human. However, a variety of Indian traditions associated with Hinduism also worship or acknowledge full or partial manifestations (known as *avatars*) of divinity into human or animal forms. The best-known textual support for such doctrines comes from the statement in the Bhagavad Gita in which Krishna states: 'whenever truth declines and the purpose of life is forgotten, I manifest myself on earth. I am born in every age to protect the good, to destroy evil, and to re-establish truth'.

Inclusivist   A religion or movement within a religion that acknowledges that the TRUTH-CLAIMS of other religions regarding doctrines and practices that express the true nature of divinity and its relation to the human, are also relevant or alternatively valid expressions of reality. (*See also* EXCLUSIVISM; PLURALISM; UNIVERSALISM)

Inculturation   Traditionally used to describe the process whereby a dominant religion adapts itself to local understandings, most early work on inculturation looked at Christian missionary activity. Much of the study of inculturation explores how SACRED SYMBOLS can provide resistance against the power of colonizers and dominant groups. Today, the study of inculturation has to take account of the movement of populations and the transmigration of religion into new environments. (*See also* SYNCRETISM)

Indigeneity   Sometimes referred to as indigenism, the term indicates one of the polarized positions in POST-COLONIAL studies. In opposition to HYBRIDITY, indigeneity explores the range of cultural and religious strategies that emphasize difference, authenticity of tradition and the assertion of self-determination and purity or superiority. Indigeneity concerns attempts by religious and cultural groups to recover local traditions undefiled by the colonial or foreign contact. Such examples of indigeneity would be the emergence of Hindutva, which asserts that the indigenous religion of India is Hinduism, or alternatively some forms of Islamic revivalism.

Indigenous Religion   A contemporary label for religions which have existed as the original location of religious identity in any one society. Such religions may be small-scale, kept within the confines of a village or tribal society, and continue to remain in spite of forces of colonialism or GLOBALIZATION. On the other hand, they may be revivals of ancient traditions that pre-existed domination by one of the world religions. Indigenous religions have also been labelled PRIMITIVE, PRIMAL and PRE-LITERATE. Each of these labels is problematic for various reasons.

Initiation A single RITUAL or series of rites that introduce a man or a woman into religious life. Although predominantly the domain of young males, there are initiation rites for young women too. The usual purpose of initiation rites is to move the initiate from the profane to the SACRED sphere, and allow him/her to maintain access to such realms throughout adult life. Initiation ceremonies bring about the death of the old self and lead the person into his/her new purified self, accepted by the deity and the religious community of worshippers. (*See also* RITES OF PASSAGE)

Inspiration A term used in the religious sense to express a condition, event or writing that does not occur merely by human achievement but is the product of some kind of meeting or encounter of the human spirit or intuition with the divine. In Christianity, for example, REVELATION of Scripture is regarded as a product of inspiration. Islam sharply distinguishes revelation and inspiration, as revelation ceased with the Qur'an but the inspiration of sainthood (*wilayat*) continued.

Institutionalization The process whereby a religious movement creates and maintains formal structures in order to realize its values and goals and to consolidate itself within society. Institutionalization can bring advantages of continuity and organization but often at the loss of spontaneity and COMMUNITAS, and eventually leading to stagnation and possibly fragmentation. The typical response to such processes is breakaway revival movements attempting to restore the original motivations or experiences of the founding generation. (*See also* CHARISMA)

Insufflation A practice found in many religions, including Christianity, Islam and Indian traditions, whereby the spirit of the deity is passed to the person through blowing or breathing. It is usually found in exorcist or healing practices. (*See also* EXORCISM)

Integration   A policy towards migrant communities maintained in societies where MULTICULTURALISM or PLURALISM underlies government policy. Integration acknowledges distinct differences of religion, dress, diet and other cultural practices, acknowledging that diversity is something to be celebrated. Citizenship can be negotiated in a number of diverse ways that cater to the differences of minority communities. (*See also* ASSIMILATION)

Intellectionist Theory   A theoretical position that understands religion to be a way of explaining the world as opposed to symbolism which perceives religion to be a symbolic language functioning to make statements about the social ordering of society.

Interiority   A state of defensive isolation maintained by a community or a religious group to protect it from contamination by a powerful or impure 'other'. Interiority can arise as a reaction to invasion, colonial domination, religious persecution, forms of exploitation from outside or a sense of religious 'specialness' that requires protection from 'ungodly' or 'impure' forces. (*See also* COLONIALISM)

Intuitive Ontology   The way in which the mind constructs combinations of ontological categories such as persons, animate beings, artifacts, events and abstractions, each containing domain-specific expectations which constitute our intuitive ontology. (*See also* COUNTER-INTUITIVE)

Islamicization   A term used to refer to the contemporary worldwide phenomenon of Muslims returning to a conscious and renewed application of their religion, either for political, IDENTITY or FAITH reasons. (*See also* REVERSION)

Kismetic Also known as the pragmatic dimension, kismetic is a term created by Roger Ballard (1987) which refers to 'those ideas, practices and behavioural strategies which are used to explain the otherwise inexplicable, and if possible to turn adversity in its tracks'. In other words, the pragmatic or kismetic dimension describes a vast range of religious practices and motivations for carrying out such practices in which devotees attempt to ally the divinity with their efforts to secure good fortune in this life. Typical of such motivations would be efforts to bring about good harvests, avoid natural disasters, safeguard health and life, ensure fertility or drive away EVIL spirits. (*See also* FOLK RELIGION)

Kratophany A type of HIEROPHANY that refers to a manifestation or showing of sacred power or power that is derived from non-natural sources. Thus miracles would have to be categorized as kratophanies until such time they were proved to be caused by natural forces. However, the belief that such natural forces had divine origins would allow the scholar to utilize kratophany as a tool of analysis. (*See also* HIEROPHANY; THEOPHANY)

Laicization   A term which describes the move towards increased focus upon the laity and their significance in religious practice and organization combined with a lessening of the role of priesthoods or other kinds of religious professionals. (*See also* PRIEST)

Legitimation   A term used in the SOCIOLOGY OF RELIGION to refer to the process whereby religious followers develop strategies to ensure that an innovation in religious life is linked to an already established tradition in order for it to be perceived as divinely ordained or sanctioned. (*See also* AUTHENTICITY)

Liberation   A term used to refer to human emancipation. It is more commonly associated with Eastern traditions which share a common DOCTRINE of an ultimate and final freedom from the condition of being reborn in the mind/body realms of created or finite existence. Often liberation models are compared with the SALVATION models of Christianity, in that the former rely upon human effort through practice to achieve emancipation, whilst the latter focus on the redemptive activities of God. However, a closer look at Indian religions reveals both liberation and salvation models. (*See also* GRACE; REDEMPTION)

Liberation Theology   A form of theology and political activism influenced by the Marxist critique of religion as oppression maintained by the ruling elites over the mass of the people. Liberation theologians, particularly in South America, questioned the Roman Catholic role in supporting and maintaining the status quo whereby the dominance of small but powerful land-owning elites was perpetuated. Such theologians differed from Marxism in that they did not dismiss religion as part of the exploitation but rather developed theologies to justify action on behalf of the poor and oppressed that originated in the teachings of the Gospels.

Liminality   A term used to describe the condition of being on the threshold, between social or cultural states or in the borders between one stage of life and another. Liminal people are neither here nor there, difficult to define, outside the positions assigned by convention, ceremony, law or custom, and as such slip through the usual networks of CLASSIFICATION that normally locate individuals or groups in a cultural context. The concept of liminality is important for the study of religion in a number of contexts. Traditionally associated with stages within RITUALS that are to do with social or cultural transition, where the individual has left one stage of life but not yet fully emerged into the new stage, the liminal stage of the ritual may represent the person as possessionless, monstrous, without status and powerless. In contemporary modern societies, liminality is a useful concept to explore marginality of all types, such as new religion membership, migration processes or communities that find themselves in the borders between two dominant religions. (*See also* RITES OF PASSAGE)

Little Traditions   A term used in contrast to GREAT TRADITIONS and coined for particular application to Indian religions. It refers to local or regional forms of religion which have their own deities, RITUALS and SACRED TEXTS that are not found throughout India and that are not defined as Sanskrit culture, regarded as ORTHODOX by religious elites. The term has wider applicability in the study of religion, where local variants compete with an overarching constructed orthodoxy.

Logic   An ancient form of philosophy that deals with the art of rational and coherent argument. Classic logic has the premise, the arguments and finally the conclusion. Trained logicians examine all three stages for consistency. The PHILOSOPHY OF RELIGION has developed its own logical arguments, often to do with rationally proving the FAITH statements of DOCTRINE.

Logos Originally derived from the Greek for 'word' and applied in Christianity and Judaism to describe God's personified Word or wisdom active in creation. Most famously, the New Testament Gospel of St John describes Jesus as as a pre-existent Logos, active in both the origins and maintenance of creation and incarnate as a human being. The idea of Logos as the Word of God originating creation and remaining within it as the life force or spark of God occurs within some Indian THEISTIC traditions. Islam has also developed the DOCTRINE of the 'Perfect Man' which has parallels with Christian logos THEOLOGY.

Magic   RITUAL practices performed with the intention to bring about practical gains, to control nature or supernatural beings for pragmatic consequence leading to the material or psychological benefit of the performer or the community represented by the performer. Magic has been differentiated from religion, but such approaches are simplistic and Eurocentric, stemming from the Christian distinctions between the world of spirits and the divine. However, in many other religions – Islam, for example – practices defined as magical would be focused towards Allah or his representatives. The distinction of magic and religion also acknowledges the implicit idea that magic deals with this world, whilst the motivations of religion are other-worldly. In reality, the vast majority of religious adherents throughout the world utilize the resources of their various divinities for worldly goals. (*See also* KISMETIC; PRAGMATISM)

Marginality   *See* LIMINAL.

Martyr   In both Islam and Christianity, a martyr refers to witnessing and is closely linked with the idea of the proselytizing of an exclusive divinely-given truth. Thus a sacrificial death in such activity confers on the individual a special status to be rewarded in respective after-lives, lauded in SACRED TEXTS and exemplary for those that follow in their activities. Certain situations can create cults of martyrdom and the causes and manifestations of these are of interest to the scholar of religion.

Materialism Religious WORLD-VIEWS tend to utilize the term 'materialism' in two different ways: i) to describe the condition of a person or society that indulges in undisciplined acquisitiveness or carnality; ii) to label individuals or societies that view the world without any reference to a divine being and perceiving matter to be basic reality. (*See also* EMPIRICISM; SPIRITUALITY)

Mediation A term used to describe individuals or events that have been able to bring the two domains of the divine and the human into contact with each other. The mediator is able to channel divine power and transfer it to other human beings and thus assist to either liberate or save them from the human condition. Such figures as gurus, PRIESTS, PROPHETS, saviours, SHAMANS, saints, avatars and religious founders have all functioned to mediate between the world of the SACRED and the mundane.

Meditation A wide variety of practices used in a number of religious traditions involving either devout and continuous remembrance of a religious theme, or one-pointed focus upon a religious object, thought or inner point of concentration, which serves to deepen spiritual insight or to achieve union or intimacy with the divine being. Religions develop postures, breathing exercises, formula repetition and forms of mental discipline as aids to meditation. (*See also* CONTEMPLATION)

Menstruation Although menstruation is not in itself a manifestation of religion, attitudes towards it are shaped by religious beliefs and prejudices. Many religions regard menstruation as TABOO and observe exclusion from religious life and purification rituals to allow the woman back into the community at the end of the menstruation period. In Islam, Jainism, Judaism, some forms of Hinduism and Christianity women are denied access to religious buildings or SACRED RITUALS. Although Sikhism does not maintain an official position with regard to menstruation, women are discouraged or forbidden to publicly read the *Guru Granth Sahib* (the SACRED TEXTS) in the *gurdwara*. Orthodox Jewish women perform ritual bathing at the end of the menstruation. Explanations for menstruation taboos are many, arising from anthropological, feminist and psychological studies.

Metanarrative   An overarching story or NARRATIVE that provides an all-encompassing view of the world through which the individual filters or perceives reality. The POSTMODERNIST perception of religion is that of a metanarrative that encompasses a vast number of narratives. The basic postmodernist position is SCEPTICISM, marked by the methodological process of deconstruction of metanarrative.

Metaphor   The use of a word or phrase usually found in one context or application, with another object or action where it is not literally applicable and where it interacts to provide new meaning or understanding. Religious language is marked by the use of metaphor as a rhetorical device to deal with the inadequacy of human language to define or circumscribe the divine. However, the use of metaphor in SACRED TEXTS has developed a secondary religious discipline of interpretation. If the sacred text is perceived to be of divine origin, then the use of the metaphorical requires sophisticated EXEGESIS in order to understand correctly the divine REVELATION or message. (*See also* ANALOGY; SYMBOLS)

Metaphysics   An ancient branch of philosophy that deals with the fundamental questions of existence and the nature of existence itself. The relationship between the mind, body and spirit, the nature of the self, life after death, the meaning of existence, and the existence of ultimate reality all fall within the realm of classical metaphysics. (*See also* PHILOSOPHY OF RELIGION)

Metempsychosis   The transfer of the soul of a human being or animal into a new body of the same or different species at death. (*See also* REINCARNATION)

Methodology   The theoretical tools applied to the particular study of a religious phenomenon in order to aid analysis and reflection. In the modern study of religion there is a wide variety of methodologies that can be selected, as so many academic disciplines feed into the subject. The choice of methodology will say as much about the WORLD-VIEW of the particular scholar as it does about the subject under study. Consequently methodologies that are utilized need to be scrutinized by scholars of religion as much as the content of the study. Modern ideas from anthropology insist that the scholar of contemporary religion is reflexive. (*See also* REFLEXIVITY)

Migration The movement of individuals and groups of individuals has always been significant for the transformation and spread of religion. Early examples of migration that have influenced religious life are Abraham, Rumi, the people of Israel, and the first Muslims. In the twentieth century, mass movements of populations have taken place as a result of colonial and POST-COLONIAL disruptions. These movements have significantly transformed the religious landscape of the world, turning some local forms of religion into global communities. (*See also* DIASPORA; ETHNICITY; GLOBALIZATION)

Millenarian A type of religious movement that arises with a particular emphasis on the imminent end of the human race or the destruction of the world. Classic millenarian movements have arisen throughout the history of Christianity, responding to the prophetic visions of the Book of Revelations concerning the return of Jesus Christ at the end of the world. The term itself takes its name from the belief in a thousand years of peace and justice that will take place after the APOCALYPTIC disasters. Such groups tend to surface in times of uncertainty and human tragedy. However, the term millenarian has been extended to cover movements arising in other religions which have comparable myths of the end time. (*See also* CARGO CULTS)

Miracle The ability of a divine or supernatural being or its agent to perform actions which appear to violate the rules or laws of nature. The vast majority of religious NARRATIVES contain miraculous events which function to maintain awe for the sacred in the mind of the believer. Religions also utilize miracles to compete with alternative WORLD-VIEWS, especially other religions, in order to demonstrate superiority. (*See also* HAGIOGRAPHY)

Model   A methodology of study introduced into the study of religion from the social sciences whereby theorizing is aided by contrasting or describing the phenomena under study with a simpler system whose properties are already known or understood. (*See also* ANALOGY; PARADIGM)

Modernism   A term which refers to: i) groups of Roman Catholic scholars who were united by their belief that the Church needed to come to terms with scientific, critical and historical developments which marked the Western world in the post-Enlightenment era of modernity; ii) a position taken towards the industrial, scientific and technological development of the post-Enlightenment Western world and its subsequent SECULARIZATION which positively endorses the changes as progress. Early- and mid-twentieth-century forms of modernism idealistically considered scientific progress to contain the solutions to human dilemmas and existential problems. (*See also* MODERNITY; POSTMODERNISM)

Modernity   A condition of society where the traditional and miraculous WORLD-VIEW of religion has been replaced by an empirical scientific viewpoint, where people look to the latter rather than the former to solve their problems. (*See also* EMPIRICISM; MODERNISM; SECULARIZATION)

Monism   A system of viewing the world that does not perceive duality. Monism regards the world – matter, mind and spirit – to be one unity or being. The term can also be used in referring to a way of perceiving the human being which regards it as a single unified entity. It can be used in a general sense to describe any intuitive perception of unity in all things, particularly experience of the world and the person. (*See also* DUALISM; MONOTHEISM; PANTHEISM)

Monolatry   The confinement of worship to only one God although it is acknowledged that others exist. Some scholars have argued that it is a necessary stage in the transition from POLYTHEISM to MONOTHEISM. However, it exists in various forms of Indian traditions without such a transition occurring. (*See also* HENOTHEISM)

Monotheism   The worship of one God regarded as the sole and universal creator of the universe, typically expressed in the religions of Judaism, Islam and Christianity. However, varieties of monotheism can also be found in Indian traditions. Monotheistic beliefs classically assert that such a deity is personal, caring for and involving itself in the affairs of human beings through REVELATION. (*See also* DEISM; HENOTHEISM; MONISM; POLYTHEISM)

Moral Theology   A term used by Anglican and Roman Catholic theologians for the study of ethics and ethical questions as seen through the prism of Christian teachings and WORLD-VIEW. (*See also* ETHICS; THEOLOGY)

Multiculturalism   Multiculturalism is more than simply a number of diverse religions and cultures co-existing in one nation state; rather, it reflects the official policies and attitudes towards that reality. It can be defined as the political accommodation of minorities, both ethnic and religious, in a way that respects difference and is concerned with societal integration as part of nation building. (*See also* ASSIMILI-ATION; INTEGRATION; PLURALISM)

Mystery religions   Forms of redemptive religions, usually used in the context of the Hellenistic pre-Christian world, where secret rites or RITUALS were revealed by a process of INITIATION and purification in order to provide the initiate with REDEMPTION from the limitations of human existence through access to the domain of a divine entity. (*See also* GNOSTICISM)

Mysticism   Types of religious EXPERIENCE where the individual feels a loss of ego-self and a sense of oneness or unity with either a personal God or a universal consciousness. Types of mysticism exist in all the world's major religious traditions and consequently the phenomenon has generated a DISCOURSE which claims that such experiences are the under-lying essential unity of religions lying behind cultural differences or various COSMOLOGIES. Mysticism has also generated considerable interest from psychology seeking to understand how neurology correlates with such experiences. (*See also* PANENHENIC; PERENNIAL PHILOSOPHY)

Mystification   A term first used in the context of religion by Karl Marx (1818–83) and borrowed by social science approaches to the study of religion. Mystification refers to the conscious or unconscious use of credulity to hide exploitation by transforming it into a religious COSMOLOGY or IDEOLOGY that is perceived by the actors to be beneficial and part of the SACRED realm. A typical form of mystification would be the ideal of the sacred king or the ruler as the representative of the gods. However, it needs to be remembered that very often the rulers were also as mystified as the ruled.

Myth   A story of divine or SACRED significance through which truths about the world are elaborated or formulated. One kind of myth is the creation tale but myths can consist of important events in the history of the religion that take on significance beyond the mere retelling of the facts – in other words, take on a symbolic meaning. Myths are often concerned with overcoming time – for example, stories of sacred events that took place in a distant time, where in some way the divine was encountered, are retold and reinterpreted in a present made sacred by their retelling. Myths are often acted out in RITUAL, taking on a new symbolic meaning that may not have been present in the original event. Some myths are about future events, such as the return or coming of a special sacred person or god to the earth in order to transform or save the world. (*See also* DEMYTHOL-OGIZATION)

Mythology   The traditional stories of a people or culture which tell of the gods and their relation to human beings or supernatural explanations for physical phenomena. Mythologies often tell of incredible things and thus the meaning of MYTH has become associated with untrue stories, but more significantly a body of myth provides a way of explaining the world within a framework of religious truth. Contemporary studies of mythology tend to be STRUCTURALIST, in that they consider how myths function in shaping social behaviour.

Narrative   A term used to describe the various stories and DOCTRINES that constitute a religious COSMOLOGY and which when taken all together form the WORLD-VIEW of the believer. (*See also* METANARRATIVE)

Narrative Theology   A branch of THEOLOGY concerned with relating the insights and impressions raised by various NARRATIVES to theological issues, and, in particular to provide criteria by which such insights and the narratives which prompted them may be judged as to their truth-value. In Christian theology, narrative theology is primarily concerned with biblical stories.

Naturalism   A term not frequently used today to describe types of philosophical systems that asserted that the world is best explained through the natural sciences without any reference to the supernatural or the SACRED. (*See also* EMPIRICISM; POSITIVISM)

Natural Religion   *See* DEISM.

Natural Theology   A term used to refer to the body of knowledge concerning God which can be achieved by the intellect without the aid of REVELATION. Although generally used in the context of theological study of Christianity and the use of philosophical reasoning by Christian scholars, natural theology is also an aspect of Judaism and Islam. (*See also* DEISM; PHILOSOPHY OF RELIGION; THEODICY; THEOLOGY)

Necromancy   A complex of beliefs and practices, found within many indigenous religions and major religious traditions, concerned with contact with the spirits of the dead. (*See also* APOTROPAIC; SPIRITUALISM)

Neo-Pagan   The self-conscious application of the term 'pagan' to a cluster of contemporary religious traditions claiming to revive pre-Christian vernacular religions as a more holistic, non-patriarchal, eco-friendly alternative to the INSTITUTIONALIZED Christianity dominant in the West. (*See also* NEW AGE; PAGANISM)

Neo-Platonism   A philosophical system originating from Plotinus (205–70 CE) and his followers, positing a hierarchical system of emanations in which the ultimate and pure consciousness of the godhead manifests itself through a variety of increasingly less pure states of being until finally solidifying into matter. The quest of the human being, containing both spirit and matter, was to overcome the duality of thought and reality by the gradual RENUNCIATION of all that is specifically human until only the divine spirit of God remains. Although a deeply thought-out intellectual system, Neo-Platonism is also experiental and posited that the ABSOLUTE could be reached through mystical EXPERIENCE. Neo-Platonic ideas and practices were to have a massive impact on the development of Christianity, Judaism and Islam, especially in their respective mystical traditions. (*See also* MYSTICISM; PLATONISM)

Neoscholasticism   A term used to describe a THEOLOGICAL position amongst nineteenth- and twentieth-century Roman Catholic theologians that judged all philosophical and theological issues against the benchmark of the thought of Thomas Aquinas.

Neo-Thomism   *See* NEOSCHOLASTICISM.

New Age   An umbrella term used to describe a complex of interwoven religious and spiritual beliefs and practices that begin from the premise that a new age has begun in the twentieth century which will involve human beings in the discovery of their holistic relations with themselves, others and the cosmos. The new age will involve the loss of loyalty to religious and other forms of institution based on hierarchical or power relations and a return to the knowledge of an authentic self as the prime authority for the human being. (*See also* NEW RELIGIOUS MOVEMENTS; SPIRITUALITY)

New Religious Movements   Although originally termed to describe the proliferation of new religions that arose in Western Europe and North America in the second half of the twentieth century, the term has come to represent a growing area of study, especially amongst SOCIOLOGISTS OF RELIGION. It is true to say that new forms of religion have always been the hallmark of the world's religious life, and even before the 1970s such movements were studied as new Christian sects in the West. However the academic discipline of the study of NRMs came into existence as a consequence of the emergence of non-traditional religiosity in the counter-culture milieu at the end of the 1960s and into the 1970s. This 'new' religiosity manifested as an array of movements with their origins in all the world's major religions. The term remains problematic as it raises a number of questions concerning which movements should be included – for example, how old should they be or when do they cease to be new, or is 'newness' only a factor of transmigration from another culture? In spite of these difficulties, the term provides a more neutral definition than the label of CULT and allows scholars of religion to analyse the transformations that take place in the early stages of a religion's development. (*See also* BRAINWASHING; NEW AGE)

Nihilism   A term which means 'belief in nothing' and is often used to describe the condition of rejection of all ethical and religious principles. It is also used to signify the spiritual dangers inherent in certain conditions of mind such as boredom, cynicism, emptiness where loss of meaning penetrates the human affective condition. Inaccurately, it can sometimes be found to refer to Eastern philosophies which regard the world as unreal. (*See also* ATHEISM)

Nominalism   Used more narrowly in the exploration of a religion's name and how such names are ascribed, nominalism, in the wider application, is used to describe a particular methodology which focuses exclusively on discrete world faiths with rigid borders between them, defined by separate origins, histories, beliefs and practices. Nominalism can lead to a WORLD-VIEW which perceives other religious traditions as rivals to the dominant national culture. (*See also* ESSENTIALISM)

Non-Theism   A more accurate way of defining religions which do not believe in a personal deity, or, in the case of Buddhism, any unchangeable, eternal creator-force. In Indian religions, a number of ORTHODOX schools of philosophy, now described under the umbrella of Hinduism, did not originally acknowledge a personal creator-God as the source of creation. Sometimes, these religious WORLD-VIEWS are described inaccurately as ATHEISTIC. Non-theistic is the more accurate description of such movements and traditions.

Numen   A term used for a local deity or god who presides over a city, region or people.

Numinous   A term coined by Rudolf Otto (1869–1937) that stresses the holiness and the otherness of the divine and defined by him as the heart of religion. Otto explained the numinous as an experience felt in contact with *mysterium tremendum et fascinans*, something mysterious, awe-inspiring and fascinating. The appropriate response to such an experience is worship and expressions of adoration. The numinous experience is essentially one derived from contact with the transcendent and as such differs from the mystical. (*See also* IMMANENCE; MYSTICISM; TRANSCENDENCE)

O

Objectivity A position taken by some scholars of religion influenced by POSITIVISM, arguing that such study should be objective, neutral and value-free. Recent methodological positions, arising especially from the discipline of anthropology, have challenged the possibility of objectivity in the study of religion and have instead argued that the researcher openly and consciously position him/herself in the research. (*See also* REFLEXIVITY)

Obscurantism A term used in the PHILOSOPHY OF RELIGION to describe religious opposition to the secular reasoning of the Enlightenment and post-Enlightenment period in the West.

Occasionalism A term that describes a METAPHYSICAL or THEOLOGICAL position that denies causality between things based on any inherent qualities but rather attributes direct causal activity to God. Results take place when certain conditions are met only through the ordained will of God.

Occidentalism A reaction to ORIENTALISM in which African and Asian scholars reject most Western scholarship as formed within the power relations of colonialism and revolt against the global civilization dominated by the West. This negative DISCOURSE against the West and Western scholarship can be as misinformed as the orientalism that it rebelled against. A central discourse of occidentalism considers the category of religion itself to be a Western construct.

Ontological Argument   A philosophical argument for the existence of God based on the premise that the existence of the idea of God necessarily involves the existence of God. Early examples of ontological arguments were put forward by al-Kindi (801–73) and St Anselm (1033–1109). (*See also* COSMOLOGICAL ARGUMENT)

Ontologism   A philosophical system which asserts that God is the guarantor of the validity of human ideas – in other words, human knowledge is a mode of truth made possible because of an intuition or apprehension of the omniscient knowledge of God. The most basic knowledge of all, that is, knowledge of existence, is a direct perception of divine or absolute being.

Ontology   A branch of metaphysics or philosophy that deals with the nature of being.

Orientalism   A term coined by Edward Said (1935–2003) to refer to a way of coming to terms with the Orient, based on the special role assigned to the East by the West which creates a style of thought in which clear ontological distinctions are made between the categories of East and West, with the East perceived as 'other'. In the context of colonial relationships, this structuring of the East takes place within a power DISCOURSE in which understandings of the East are imposed by the West. Anyone from the West who studies Eastern religion and culture is by definition an orientalist. (*See also* OCCIDENTALISM; SUBALTERN)

Orthodox   A position which defines belief in adherence to the fundamental truths of a religious tradition. The problem for the scholar of religion is determining which position is ORTHODOX. Where CREEDS and dogmas are institutionally established by formal processes, orthodoxy is more easily determined, but not all religions are marked by such processes. In addition, all religions demonstrate considerable diversity where orthodoxy is contested. In Judaism and Christianity, orthodoxy takes on precise meaning as the proper name for particular traditions within the wider movement who laid claim to the title of 'Orthodox'. (*See also* HERESY; HETERODOX)

Orthopraxy A term that signifies correct practice. There are some religions that consider detailed knowledge and application of RITUALS and ceremonies to be more significant than holding correct beliefs concerning the nature of divinity. However, it should be remembered that what constitutes correct practice may be highly contested. For example, Shi'a and Sunni Muslims hold to different variations of the ritual PRAYER positions, but both groups would consider themselves to be upholding the correct practice. Religious traditions call upon SACRED TEXTS and time-honoured precedent to affirm the authentic nature of such practices and insist that they are ORTHODOX. (*See also* AUTHENTICITY)

Paganism   A term applied by Christians to describe the non-Christian world around them in the formative years of Christian growth. The term literally means 'country dwellers' and as such referred to the practices and beliefs of vernacular or popular religions of Europe and the Mediterranean world. Once Christianity became dominant, such traditions were suppressed or subsumed and the use of the term 'pagan' became derogatory, suggesting something either EVIL or superstitious. (*See also* APOTROPAIC; NEO-PAGAN)

Panenhenic   A term coined by R. C. Zaehner (1913–74) to categorize experiences where individuals feel a loss of individual self and a powerful sense of unity with nature. It is also referred to as 'nature mysticism'. (*See also* MYSTICISM; PERENNIAL PHILOSOPHY)

Panentheism   The view that everything exists within God, but which is distinguished from PANTHEISM, in that it acknowledges that God continues to exist outside the parameters of the universe. (*See also* MONISM)

Pantheism   The belief that one supreme being occupies the natural universe rather than existing beyond its confines. Consequently everything is the appearance of God or one single reality and God and nature are in essence one being. It can be divided into acosmic pantheism, the view that sees God as the ultimate reality, the world therefore being unreal or illusionary, or immanentist pantheism, the view that sees God as part of the world and existent within it. (*See also* IMMANENCE; MONISM)

Pantheon A term which has come to refer to a collective of go
goddesses present in a particular POLYTHEISTIC religion. The o
Pantheon was a building created in Rome for the worship of
gods.

Panthic Panthic refers to a type of religious organization, us
associated with North Indian devotional traditions, Sufism, or
other movement where a group of followers organize themselv
promote and follow the teachings of a spiritual master, living
dead. The overriding motive is usually concerned with clo
proximity or experience of the divine through mystical union. (
also DHARMIC; KISMETIC; QAUMIC)

Parable Derived from the Greek word *parabolē,* parables are stori
with hidden meanings unique to the Old Testament, the words
Jesus described in the Bible, and NARRATIVES in some Eastern religiou
traditions. C. H. Dodd (1884–1973) classically defined the parabl
as 'a metaphor or simile drawn from nature or common life
arresting the hearer by its vividness or strangeness and leaving the
mind in sufficient doubt about its precise application to tease it
into active thought'. (*See also* ANALOGY; METAPHOR; MYTH)

Paradigm Although sometimes used as an alternative to 'model' or
'theory', the term 'paradigm' was originally used by T. S. Kuhn
(1922–96) to signify a set of assumptions, insights and techniques
or practices which set the parameters of a puzzle and its solution
Kuhn argued that science works through a number of 'paradigm
shifts' after a set of discoveries results in revolution of the prevailin
WORLD-VIEW. The term 'paradigm shift' is commonly used b
commentators on religion to describe such transformations in worl
view occurring in the religious domain as a result of crisis arisi
from internal or external conflict. (*See also* MODEL)

Participant Observation A type of fieldwork where the researc
immerses him/herself in the world under observation by fully pa
ipating in the life under study. Participant observation can be ca
out either with or without the knowledge of the religious gro

however, covert observation raises ethical problems, especially as certain religions may have RITUALS, ceremonies or practices which they do not want outsiders to participate in. (*See also* ANTHROPOLOGY; ETHNOGRAPHY)

Pastoral Theology   Derived from the Latin word for 'shepherd', this branch of Christian theology concerns itself with the functions and theory of ordained ministry, the moral and spiritual requirements, functions and duties, and the care of individual parishioners with regard to counselling and other pastoral needs. In Catholic circles, pastoral theology focuses on the work of the Church and its emphasis on ministry, whereas twentieth-century Protestantism has tended to focus on individual care.

Patriarchy   A term signifying universal or collective male dominance. In feminist theory, the term provides the possibility to comprehend gender inequality as a feature of society, and to develop a critique which maintains that women's oppression is distinct from other forms of oppression. In the study of religion, patriarchy is a useful concept to understand the universal dominance of men in almost all religious forms of life, especially in the public and social spheres. (*See also* ANDROCENTRISM; FEMINISM; GENDER)

Patristics   The study of the body of texts deriving from the church fathers or bishops and scholars of the early Church in its first four or five centuries. However, the ORTHODOX Church extends the patristic period into the medieval period.

Penance   A term which refers in the Christian context to acts which mark an inner return to God or public return to the Church after a misdeed, HERESY or sin. Such acts evolved into a highly developed set of penitential disciplines which could continue for years. In contemporary Christianity, penance is mostly subsumed in the act of confession. Penance is found in a number of religions and can be a motivation for a variety of religious activities ranging from retreats, periods of PRAYER, fasting, PILGRIMAGE and ascetic practices. (*See also* ASCETICISM)

Perennial Philosophy   A phrase coined by Aldous Huxley (1894–1963) to describe his belief that mystical experiences are essentially the same in different religions, and that such experiences constitute the essence of religion, continuing as a kind of constant truth across history and cultures. The various world religions exist merely as the consequences of various interpretations placed upon such experiences. (*See also* MYSTICISM)

Perfection   A number of religious traditions posit the ideal of a transformed and purified human condition which is described in absolute terms as perfection. Such states are usually associated with the end goals of a religion and may be either an expansion or submission of the self into the higher reality of a personal and perfect deity. NON-THEISTIC traditions can also posit ideal or perfect states of consciousness in which the human being achieves complete identity with an absolute and perfect state of being – for example, the Buddhist ideal of *Nirvana*.

Phenomenology of Religion   The phenomenology of religion is distinct from the philosophical concept of phenomenology that was developed by Husserl (1859–1938); however, it borrows from Husserl the idea of 'bracketing', empathy and reduction to essences. Contemporary phenomenology in the study of religion is identified by these three characteristics: i) eidetic reduction, where religions or religious phenomena are grouped or arranged into patterns for coherence; ii) an attempt to bracket out one's own personal beliefs in order to achieve neutrality or impartiality; and iii) an attempt to enter into the world of the believer to provide an understanding of their WORLD-VIEW. (*See also* DIMENSIONAL APPROACH; EIDETIC VISION; EMPATHY)

Philology   The text-centred study of language in which the scholar sets out to make texts in other languages accessible across cultures. Words and phrases are contextualized, often in extensive footnotes, within works of translation. Any text, including sacred texts, requires an understanding of: i) the relations between textual units; ii) other texts written within the same culture, especially those of the same genre; iii) the intentions of the author especially in regard to readership; and iv) events taking place in the wider milieu at the time of composition. Some philologists have studied the constraints on text construction which limit or determine the form, shape or content of the final product.

Philosophy of Religion   How philosophy of religion is defined depends entirely on the university department in which the subject is studied. For the student in a Philosophy department, the approach is likely to be concerned with the problems of coherence and consistency involved in maintaining a concept of God. The Religious Studies student is more likely to find the phrase used to describe the intellectual content of a religion, the rational formulation of its doctrines into a coherent WORLD-VIEW. The student of THEOLOGY will study philosophical ideas to obtain a rational understanding of REVELATION or a better comprehension of doctrines, the ultimate objective a better grasp of theology.

Pietism   A Protestant movement to restore religion through condemning over-emphasis on DOCTRINE and philosophy through advocating PRAYER circles and devotion. The term has spread into the study of other religions and loosely refers to movements and individuals who practise a QUIETIST and devotional religion, avoiding politics, intellectualism and scholarly theological speculation.

Pilgrimage   Journeys undertaken by individuals or groups to SACRED places in order to obtain supernatural help, either in solving the dilemmas of everyday life, seeking cures for afflictions, or to make vows, either as an act of thanksgiving or as penance. Pilgrimage may be required as a central act of the religion, as in Islam, or it may be an extra act of piety, as in Christianity or Hinduism. Typical places of pilgrimage are associated variously with events in the lives of sacred people, places where the divine is believed to have manifested, or tombs of saints and founders. Pilgrimage centres are HIEROPHANIES, as defined by Mircea Eliade (1907–86), places where divinity is believed to have revealed itself on Earth, and such places constitute a sacred geography within a religious tradition.

Platonism   A school of philosophy originating with the ideas of Plato (427–347 BCE), an Athenian student of Socrates. Plato asserted that the soul naturally directs itself towards the good and that wrong-doing exists because of a mistaken presumption concerning what is good. The central aim of existence is to cultivate insight into the nature of goodness, truth and beauty. The soul has knowledge of these ultimate values because it recollects from the world of sense experience back to the true or higher world of eternal forms. By apprehending these forms, the soul attains a state of well-being. Theologically, Plato posited the existence of a demiurge who creates the world from his own forms and thus enables it to participate in his perfection by the inclusion of the soul. Plato's ideas were to have a significant impact on the development of Judaism, and on Christianity from the early period of the church fathers through to the renaissance. It would later influence Islamic philosophy and MYSTICISM. (*See also* NEO-PLATONISM)

Pluralism   Religious pluralism refers to the existence of two or more religions within a given territory. It is usually associated with a society, religion or culture that acknowledges that the differences of practice and belief in the various traditions that co-exist with each other are legitimate, and claims to sole truth cannot be advanced on behalf of one tradition over another. However, it needs to be borne in mind that such ideal states of co-existence rarely exist and the study of religious pluralism tends to focus on areas where such consensus breaks down. (*See also* ECLECTICISM; EXCLUSIVITY; INCLUSIVITY; SYNCRETISM)

Poiesis   An anthropological term borrowed from Aristotle (384–322 BCE) which signifies the way a religion is examined as something crafted or made. Such an approach will often analyse COSMOLOGIES through the examination of SYMBOLS and rhetoric.

Polytheism   Religions which worship more than one god. However, the term polytheism was coined by missionaries or scholars who regarded such traditions as a lesser or more primitive expression of religion than MONOTHEISM. More recent scholarship requires a deeper understanding and empathy with polytheism and the COSMOLOGIES that sustain it. Polytheism may consist of veneration of a vast array of local deities or of a PANTHEON of gods given ANTHROPOMORPHIC qualities, as in ancient Greece or Vedic India. Many apparent polytheistic religions also maintain belief in a supreme universal creator-god who may have brought the gods into existence or of whom the gods themselves are merely aspects or attributes. (*See also* ANIMISM; HENOTHEISM)

Popular culture   The interest in popular culture for scholars of religion relates to the impact of religious movements on the production, content and use of the media of popular culture. Religion has always impacted on architecture, music, dance, painting, literature and other cultural artifacts. However, although earlier cultures may have been organized with religion as a central feature, this may not be the case in contemporary Western societies. If popular culture is defined as art, entertainment and cultural objects that have proved to be successful in gathering significant audiences outside of elite groups, then the question has to be asked by scholars of religion to what degree such cultural artifacts continue to carry religious SYMBOLS or messages, and in what way such messages have been transformed. (*See also* AESTHETICS)

Positivism   A term used to describe a movement or a METHODOLOGY that claims that knowledge cannot exist outside the realm of the scientifically verifiable, and therefore rejects religious statements of belief in a being that lies beyond empirical evidence as meaningless. (*See also* EMPIRICISM)

Post-colonial   The continuation of colonial relations even after independence movements restored national freedom to colonized nations. Post-colonial theory is based on the premise that the formerly colonized remain under the economic and political domination of the West. Post-colonial theory underlies much of the analysis of FUNDAMENTALIST movements in Muslim nations or South Asia, where such movements are seen as asserting religious identities as part of nationhood in opposition to the GLOBALIZATION of Western culture and consumerism.

Postmodernism   With regard to the study of religion, postmodernism is best understood as RELATIVISM and a lack of sympathy towards the concept of objectivity. Thus we find notions that everything is 'text' to be deconstructed or decoded and the basic material of such texts or constructions is meaning. Postmodernism is defined by Jean-François Lyotard (1924–98) as 'incredulity towards all METANARRATIVES' and arises from Western societies being involved in a process of ever-increasing transformations which can no longer sustain a paradigm of progress. Postmodernism impacts on the study of religion in two distinct ways: i) in the analysis of the conditions of postmodernist society itself and the impact it has on both the emergence of new forms of religion and existing traditions; ii) on the methodologies used to study religion, most significantly in questioning how knowledge is produced. Religious scholars typically defined as postmodernist are self-critical and resistant to the overarching dominance of metanarratives, defined as theories or all-embracing world-views typical of religious cosmologies.

Practical Theology   The branch of theology concerned with the interaction of DOCTRINE and behaviour. Contemporary forms of the discipline focus on theoretical engagement or critical theological reflection on Christian practice. The key factor of the discipline is critical dialogue with theory and practice.

Pragmatism   A test of truth developed by William James (1842–1910), who stated that ideas are true only if they can be verified and corroborated. The meaning of all assumptions can only be evaluated by looking at their practical results or application. Thus religious experiences can be explained in terms of the way that they impact on life and determine behaviour. John Dewey (1859–1952) insisted that religious ideas should always be associated with practical actions and not with an ultimate authority. Pragmatism came to be influential in the study of both religion and philosophy.

Prayer   A mental or vocal expression to a deity or power of absolute value, common to most of the world's religions. Prayer can be in adoration, thanksgiving, penitential or petitionary, either individual or communal, formal or informal, and all these are common to most religions but each individual tradition may emphasize particular forms of prayer over another, or maintain that their form of prayer is unique on the basis of their individual COSMOLOGIES or DOCTRINES. (*See also* CONTEMPLATION; MEDITATION)

Praxis Used as a religious term to refer to the vast and varied body of practices that constitute religious activity, such as RITUALS, ceremonies, PILGRIMAGES, worship, social acts, dress codes and special diets. Praxis is sometimes used in contrast to DOCTRINE, as in ORTHO-PRAXY as opposed to ORTHODOXY.

Predestination The DOCTRINE that God knows and ordains all actions and events before they occur, having determined them from the origin of time. In Christianity it occurs in the debate as to whether God already ordained who is redeemed. In other religions the argument has focused around free-will issues. (*See also* DETERMINISM)

Pre-existence The belief that a founder of a religion existed prior to their human birth as an eternal being. Although typically applied to Jesus Christ, variations on the ideal exist in Islam and Buddhism with regard to their respective founders.

Pre-literate Religion A term sometimes used to describe indigenous religions but which is problematic in a number of ways – perhaps the most significant is that many indigenous religions are no longer non-literate but utilize the Internet and other texts very effectively in order to defend their traditions against threats. The term also privileges literacy over oral and other means of communication and sets up a false dichotomy with 'world religions' that own a corpus of SACRED TEXTS. (*See also* INDIGENOUS RELIGION; PRIMAL RELIGION; PRIMITIVE RELIGION)

Premodernism A term used to group together the characteristics of a society that was or remains in the traditional forms of organization, religious practice and belief that existed prior to modernization or industrialization. There is an evolutionary assumption in the term which suggests that societies will progress from premodern to modern and then to postmodern. However, this assumes a development that parallels Western nations and their unique history after the Enlightenment. (*See also* MODERNITY; POSTMODERNISM)

Priest   A religious functionary who has the power to officiate between the deity and worshippers, able to act as an intermediary. In religious traditions where priests are required, it is part of the COSMOLOGY that ordinary worshippers are not able to approach the divinity without the intervention of a specialist given particular authority. In Hinduism, priests owe their status to their birth within an elite caste group; in Christianity, their authority is based on tradition, training and apostolic succession which allows them to inherit the authority of Jesus Christ. Priests may maintain their authority through their access to SACRED TEXTS, holy sites, religious languages, or performance of RITUALS.

Primal Religion   A term used for 'PRIMITIVE RELIGION' that is considered to overcome the negative connotations of the latter. However, the term 'primal' still suggests, as does the variation 'archaic', that the traditions are somehow outdated or belonging to museums rather than transforming and dynamic expressions of lived religion. It also suggests that the traditions involved are about to be replaced by either more 'advanced' world systems such as Western rationality or one of the world religions. (*See also* INDIGENOUS RELIGIONS; PRE-LITERATE RELIGIONS)

Primitive Religion   A term used by early anthropologists to describe the religious forms of 'primitive' human societies. Emile Durkheim (1858–1917) defined primitive religion as requiring two conditions. The first was that the religion must be found in societies whose organization was nowhere exceeded, and the second was that the religion must be explainable without recourse to any element from a preceding religion. Durkheim's stated intention for the study of such religions was to arrive at an understanding of the contemporary through tracing the religious nature of humankind back to its origins. The term is no longer considered to be politically correct and has been replaced by 'PRIMAL RELIGION'. (*See also* INDIGENOUS RELIGION; PRE-LITERATE RELIGION)

Primordialism A position taken towards ETHNICITY that sees it as fixed and determined by rigid boundaries based on blood and kinship, in which an individual receives certain unchangeable attributes at birth which are reinforced by socialization into the group's customs, language and religion. (*See also* CONSTRUCTIVISM; SITUATIONALISM)

Privatized Religion A phrase coined in SECULARIZATION theory to posit that in modern societies, religion moves into the domain of the individual's private life and becomes a matter of personal choice, as opposed to its role in public and social life in traditional societies where it is more prescribed. (*See also* SECULARIZATION)

Process Theology Broadly defined, it refers to any theology which emphasizes process or becoming in the nature of humankind and considers that God continues to develop through His relationship with a changing world. Process theology focuses on relationship rather than being. (*See also* PRAGMATISM)

Projection Theory The idea that gods and divinity are projections of human desires and needs or the objectification of human nature. Forms of projection theory can be found in the attitude towards religion posited by Karl Marx (1818–83) and Sigmund Freud (1856–1939) but Tibetan Buddhism is also projectionist in that it explains that the gods and demons perceived after death are merely projections of the human mind.

Prophecy In a general sense, 'prophecy' can be used to define any human statement which is inspired by a divine or transcendent source. Prophecy has had a major role in Zoroastrianism, Judaism, Christianity and Islam but examples of it can be found in the THEISTIC elements of Indian traditions. Prophecy in the Jewish and Christian traditions usually calls for changes in behaviour, challenges existing religious, social or political order, or promotes a deeper awareness of relation with the divine and the role of humankind within such relations. Prophecy is not divination or the prediction of future events, other than in the specific sense of utterances that claim that the relationship of humans to the divine will be radically changed in the future or warnings concerning the fate of humankind if obedience does not occur. (*See also* PROPHET)

Prophet   Figures associated with the ability to utter PROPHECY. Sociologically, Max Weber (1864–1920) defined the prophet as someone invested with charismatic authority who challenges existing religious institutions. In Jewish and Christian traditions, the typical prophet criticizes existing religious and political institutions with the authority of God, even though the institutions under challenge may have been started originally by the same deity. Prophets claim individual authority from God, expressed in their utterances and miracles, rather than the institutional authority of priests. Islam has generated a substantial literature on the function of the prophet as part of the centrality of that role within that religious tradition, where they exist as the primary intermediary of REVELATION, the means for communicating God's will and plan for human beings and warning against the perils of disobedience.

Providence   Although strictly used theologically to refer to God's prior knowledge of the world and its needs, the term is usually used to describe the role of the MONOTHEISTIC God in the government of nature, humankind and history. In Christianity, Judaism and Islam, God not only works through the natural order but is also involved in the linear working-out of a divine destiny throughout history.

Psychology of Religion   A discipline for the study of religion that views religion primarily as relations between body, emotions and psyche with no reference to the existence of supernatural beings or God. Historically, psychology has had the tendency to reduce religion to infantile or confused behaviour, and has been concerned with the nature and origin of religious EXPERIENCE.

Qaumic 'Qaumic' is a term used by Roger Ballard to describe the more recent phenomenon in Indian religions where a group of people use a set of religious ideas and activities to close ranks as a community and advance their common social, economic and political interests. (*See also* COMMUNALISM)

Queer Theology A method of analysis that emerged in the 1990s for exploring the history of gender difference in terms of sexual outlaws and outcasts working in coalition against heterosexual normativity. Queer theology draws upon queer theory, a social constructivist position, positing the view that heterosexuality is not natural but rather constructed differently in different times and cultures. In queer theology, difference is celebrated as an insight into truth. (*See also* FEMINISM; GENDER)

Quietism A term coined in the seventeenth century to describe forms of Christian spirituality where the individual believes that no amount of human effort can reach to God. In order to reach the divine, the soul simply rests in the presence of God with perfect FAITH. Self-abnegation and annihilation of the will are taken to the point of ceasing even to care about one's own SALVATION. Quietism has come into the language of Religious Studies to describe any religious group whose spirituality minimizes human activity in favour of GRACE, and features the ideal of self-surrender. (*See also* PIETY)

Rationalism Since the nineteenth century, associated with the type of thinking that rejects religious explanations of the world on the grounds that they are not compatible with human REASON. It is often associated with SECULARISM, HUMANISM, ATHEISM and AGNOSTICISM.

Realism Realism can be defined as: i) any form of thinking which is wary of speculation and defends the empirical observation of reality; ii) a philosophical idea that denies that the universe is constituted of CONSCIOUSNESS and argues that the external world is real. (*See also* IDEALISM)

Reason In religious DISCOURSE most discussion of reason has been in the context of its role in relation to REVELATION. There are several views in Christianity and Islam extending from those who consider reason and revelation to be incompatible to those who regard reason and revelation to be two sides of the same truth, and who consider reason to be a limited tool for discovering the nature of God and the truths of revelation. However, most religious viewpoints in these two religions perceive reason as only a means for elaborating and clarifying the ultimate form of knowledge contained in revelation rather than a superior autonomous form of knowledge to determine the nature of existence.

Recluse *See* HERMIT.

Reciprocity *See* RELIGIOUS EXCHANGE.

Recollection Various systems of meditation that have in common the use of repetition and reflection to bring to the emotions the remembrance of a deity. Recollection is usually associated with devotional traditions where intimacy or union are encouraged as a feature of a personal relationship with the deity. (*See also* CONTEMPLATION; MEDITATION; MYSTICISM; SPIRITUALITY)

Redaction Criticism A method of EXEGESIS of the Bible which examines the editorial work carried out by the authors on earlier material. (*See also* FORM CRITICISM)

Redemption A common factor in religions resulting from the human condition of subjugation or bondage to either human, natural or supernatural forces. Meaning 'buying back', redemption refers to any means through which the human being can be freed from oppression, threat or confinement, whether to body, mind or spirit, by offering up something to the supernatural in exchange for a return to a primordial condition of wholeness, freedom or safety. (*See also* LIBERATION; SALVATION)

Redistribution *See* RELIGIOUS EXCHANGE.

Reductionism A stance common to the social sciences which reduces religion to the underlying economic, social, political, geographical or psychological features which are believed to create it, and in so doing denies the reality of religious beings and experiences or the motivations of believers as a cause of social action. In leaving the world of the divine out of the picture, religion is explained away and the DISCOURSE of rational and secular HUMANISM is privileged over the religious believer. (*See also* ETIC)

Re-enchantment *See* ENCHANTMENT.

Reflexivity Used to describe the scholar's role in the research process and their self-conscious location of themselves in their research. In anthropological studies of religion the old theoretical perspective of neutrality or suspended belief is increasingly under examination. In many studies, scholars are writing reflexive accounts that locate their own attitudes towards the object of research and its impact on the research process.

Reincarnation   The belief commonly associated with Indian religions that the individual continues after death through a succession of births and deaths in various bodies in this and other worlds. Popular forms claim that the same individual soul continues from one body to another and previous existences can be remembered, especially under hypnosis.

Relativism   The idea that there is no single truth allied to any particular WORLD-VIEW which can claim to be universal. Truth is perceived as relative to the world-view and as such it is not possible to claim that any one religion is in possession of reality over and above the language that constructs its COSMOLOGY. Taken to its extremes, relativism asserts that all individuals live in their own worlds and translations from one religion or culture to another are impossible, as there is no language or universal truth that makes them translatable. (*See also* ESSENTIALISM; PHENOMENOLOGY; POSTMODERNISM; UNIVERSALISM)

Relics   The veneration of the bodies and possessions of the sacred dead such as saints, PROPHETS, pious individuals, religious founders or other men and women recognized to have lived lives of great sanctity. Most of the world's historic religions engage in some kind of veneration of relics according to the various theologies that are followed. However, in the MONOTHEISTIC religions, although prevalent, this has come under criticism for blurring the edges with IDOLATRY.

Religion a Priori   The view that religion is a sense of the divine that exists independently of religion as a social, economic or psychological construction. Thus the concept of religion, signifying awareness and response to the SACRED, exists independently and cannot be defined by reference to any other category, even though the forms of religion may be constructed socially or culturally. It is this way of thinking that has led to the study of religion possessing its own subject area rather than being consumed into social sciences. (*See also* REDUCTIONIST; RELIGIONIST)

Religion Sui Generis *See* RELIGION A PRIORI.

Religionsgeschichtliche Schule Literally 'the history of religions school', a term used to describe a late-nineteenth-century German theological school which studied parallel developments and common beliefs within Christianity and Judaism and later Christianity and Middle-Eastern religions. (*See also* RELIGIONSWISSENSCHAFT)

Religionist A label used by opponents of the religion sui generis position, who argue that religion has no essential qualities that make it different from other social and cultural structures and that it should be explored within the framework of social science causal analysis. Such theorists have labelled as 'religionists' those that consider religion to be a unique area of human experience marked by contact with sacred realms. (*See also* RELIGION A PRIORI)

Religionswissenschaft The study of religions outside of Christianity from a neutral perspective of 'what is there to be believed?' rather than 'what must I believe?' Beginning in Germany in the nineteenth century, historians of religion outside of Christianity defended themselves against the theological claim that 'he who knows one religion knows all' by asserting Max Muller's counterclaim that 'he who knows one religion knows none'. (*See also* COMPARATIVE RELIGION; RELIGIONSGESCHICHTLICHE SCHULE)

Religious Exchange A method of analysing religion that borrows from the subject discipline of economics. Religious phenomena are explored from the perspective of exchange activity. For example, RITUALS involve exchanges of both objects and the non-empirical between human beings and human beings and between human beings and gods, both as individual and communal activity. Such exchanges may be perceived as reciprocal where two parties exchange goods with each other, or as redistribution, where goods are funnelled through a central point. Thus PRAYER may be perceived as a reciprocal activity, whilst temples may be analysed as redistribution centres. As with other social science approaches, exchange activity analysis can be open to the criticism of ignoring the self-understandings of the actors who participate in religious activity. (*See also* REDUCTIONISM)

Religious Studies   Generally used for the study of religions other than Christianity and for the analysis of religion, utilizing the disciplines of the social sciences, developed into a package of study in higher education. However, it is also used to describe a method of study that draws upon social science and humanities disciplines and METHODOLOGY to study religion(s). As such, Christianity is also available to be studied utilizing such an approach rather than the traditional approach of THEOLOGY. (*See also* PHENOMENOLOGY)

Religious Traditions   A phrase used increasingly by scholars of religion to define a discrete package of religious beliefs and practices perceived by insiders to be an enclosed system. In this context, not only religions representing a WORLD-VIEW, such as Buddhism or Islam, may be defined as religious traditions, but also SECTS and sub-divisions within them. The term was introduced to replace the contentious use of 'FAITH TRADITION' but 'religious tradition' can have problems of its own, as it assumes that all religions exist by constructing a tradition based on a chain of memory. Some religious groups and movements come into existence to destroy or subvert tradition.

Renunciation   A religious position towards the world whereby an individual or group actively seek to withdraw from normal conventions of social life – for example, marriage, child-rearing, wealth, position, fame, possessions – and seek to live a lifestyle of surrender to a deity or a spiritual discipline. Such a position usually arises from a world-denying attitude within the religion, the belief that the goals of the religion are greater than those of society or that the goals of society are a distraction. (*See also* ASCETICISM; HERMIT)

Repentance   An individual's or group's regret at a past action, word or thought deemed to be unacceptable. In the MONOTHEISTIC religions, the primary act of repentance is a turning towards God and away from a previous way of life considered incomplete, unsatisfactory or unwholesome. Repentance becomes a continuous act to maintain a life in God or a life with God. (*See also* PENANCE)

Revealed Religion   A religion which originates in REVELATION. (*See also* DEISM)

Revelation   The intervention into human affairs of a personal, MONOTHEISTIC, all powerful deity in order to provide a blueprint for behaviour or as a salvationary act in order to restore or establish relations between the human and the divine, and between humans. Most revelations contain the paradox that they are revealed within a particular cultural milieu and historical epoch but simultaneously are believed to be universal and all-encompassing. The tension between these two provides the impetus for creative development of the religion over time to deal with changing situations.

Reversion   A term sometimes used by Muslims to describe the process of conversion to Islam. It is based on the doctrine that all newborn children are Muslim by virtue of being born in a condition of natural surrender to God, and with their natural or God-given state of purity intact. Therefore conversion to Islam marks a return to the primal or original religion maintained by all at birth. Reversion is also used to describe the process of Muslims returning to the practice of their religion. (*See also* ISLAMICIZATION)

Revivalism   The periodic appearance of religious movements or individuals who seek to take an existing religion back to its roots or origins in order to restore a perceived purity of DOCTRINE and practice, believing that the present condition of the religion is corrupted, institutionalized or has lost its original enthusiasm or meaning. (*See also* CHARISMA; FUNDAMENTALISM; INSTITUTIONALIZATION)

Rigorism   A philosophical term referring to any attitudes which oppose the position of compromising Christian morality with secular standards.

Rite   *See* RITUAL.

Rites of Passage   Defined by the anthropologist Arnold van Gennup (1960) as 'rites which accompany every change of place, state, social position and age'. Typical of such RITUALS would be those that mark birth, marriage and death. They can also demonstrate formal entry into a religious community. Van Gennup identified three stages to all such rituals: separation, LIMINALITY (margin) and aggregation. Separation symbolically marks departure from the earlier fixed point in the social structure; liminality demonstrates the ambiguity of the individual who is between one stage of life and another; aggregation is when the rite of passage is completed and the individual is expected to behave in accordance with the customary norms of the new stage and to obtain the rights associated with it.

Ritual   A repeated act performed ceremonially that carries with it an ultimate value, meaning, sacrality or significance for the performers and any other participants can be defined as religious ritual. Religious rituals are often associated with MYTH or the believer's view of the essential structures of the universe. For example, rituals may be performances of significant events that are believed to have taken place in the religion's origins and which carry considerable levels of SACRED meaning. The sacred time of the myth is transformed into the present through performance of such rituals. Other types of religious ritual may be concerned with seasonal cycles, RITES OF PASSAGE, liturgical calendars, or response to crises.

Sacred　A term used by scholars of religion to designate the unique qualities of the 'religious' and to indicate a dividing line between the realm of the ordinary or mundane and a special realm marked by the benevolent, or malevolent presence of a non-human power. In their DOCTRINES, some religions state that there is no division between the mundane and sacred, but, in practice, such a dividing line can always be found. (*See also* SUPERNATURAL)

Sacred Texts　The primary and secondary collections of texts considered by a religious tradition to be authentically endowed with sacredness. Primary sacred texts are those written by founders or believed to have been received through REVELATION; and secondary texts are those written as commentary or interpretation of the primary texts. Some religions distinguish between books of revelation and INSPIRATION. The former are perceived to have come direct from a divine being, whilst the latter have been written by human beings with a close relation to the divine or an elevated state of consciousness. Most of the world's major religions have closed the circle of which books can be counted as authentic sacred texts, sometimes through negotiations at councils called for that very purpose. Such collections are known as the CANON.

Sacrifice　The offering up of something to a deity in the hope that some kind of connection will be established between the sacrificer (and possibly their community) and the SACRED. Sacrifice can be done for the following reasons: i) the belief that the gods literally needed sustenance; ii) the belief that it establishes communion between the deity and worshippers; iii) as a gift to supplement PRAYERS of petition; iv) to pacify divine anger; v) to ward off evil spirits; vi) to seal a contract with the deity; vii) to offer homage or praise to the deity; viii) as an act to remove pollution and assist achieving purification. (*See also* ATONEMENT)

Sacrilege An action or utterance that violates the religious believers' sense of the SACRED as embodied in a person or object. It may consist of a profanation against a religious building or an outrage against a religious functionary – for example, an act of violence or sexual activity carried out in a religious place. An act of sacrilege will be specific to the religious beliefs of the tradition. For example, an act which performs some kind of profanity on the Qur'an is more likely to cause deep offence and be regarded as sacrilege than in a religion which considers its SACRED TEXT to have been created by human inspiration. (*See also* BLASPHEMY)

Salvation Although traditionally associated with Christianity and the saviour figure of Jesus Christ, salvation models of human emancipation can be found in some Indian THEISTIC traditions where reliance upon the GRACE of a deity is required to overcome the limitations of human effort. Buddhism also has variants of salvation models in the Amida/Amitabha cults of Japan and China. In these traditions total reliance upon and FAITH in the Amida/Amitabha Buddha is required in order for devotees to be reborn in his paradise from where Nirvana is achievable. Salvation models contrast with LIBERATION models where emancipation takes place primarily through human effort.

Sanctification An originally Christian term that refers to the process of becoming holy or making holiness. In most Christian theology, sanctification begins at baptism and continues through to the final judgement in a process of being made saints, or becoming holy. However, most THEISTIC religions have a comparative process in which holiness is transferred or acquired through a combination of human effort and divine assistance. (*See also* REDEMPTION; SALVATION)

Scepticism   Originally used to describe someone who did not believe that REASON can attain certain knowledge of how things really are. By the nineteenth century in the West, it had acquired the meaning of someone who does not fully accept Christian theological claims, as no possible proof or evidence could be offered for them. Although no longer used as a title for a particular philosophical position, scepticism remains present in the social sciences and operates as an underlying outlook that influences the methodological approach to the study of religion. (*See also* EMPIRICISM; NATURALISM; POSITIVISM; REDUCTIONISM)

Schism   A term used to describe divisions in the Church that breach its unity and create separate movements marked by mutual hostility. The term is available for use in the analysis of other religious traditions. (*See also* HERESY)

Scholasticism   A development in Western Christianity often associated with Thomas Aquinas (1225–74), although it more accurately describes a six-century period that began with the end of the PATRISTIC period in the eighth century, and whose distinguishing mark is the use of LOGIC or REASON to provide evidence for the existence of God. The impetus for such work was the arrival in Western thought of the works of Aristotle (384–22 BCE), providing the METHODOLOGY of a more systematic use of philosophy to aid theological speculation. The scholastics are best known for their debates on the relationship between reason and FAITH, and similar arguments can be located within Islam at the same period, also inspired by contact with Greek philosophy.

Sect   Sometimes used to describe a body of persons who are agreed upon a set of religious practices and beliefs, but more precisely used to indicate a group that has divided away from a larger religious grouping and developed a distinctive body of practices and DOCTRINES which it holds to be superior to those of the religion from which it has departed. The followers may consider that they maintain the practices and doctrines in a pure form, closer to the religion's founders. From the perspective of the wider tradition, sects are perceived to be unorthodox or nonconformist. Sectarian membership is usually elective and such movements have a difficulty retaining their original fervour across generations, often leading to breakaway movements from within the sect, claiming similar reasons for SCHISM as the original founder movement. (*See also* CULT; HERESY)

Secularism   An IDEOLOGICAL position which advocates the weakening or elimination of religious influence in state and social institutions, especially education. Students of religion need to assess whether SECULARIZATION theorists, who advocate a decline in religious activity or belief, do not themselves maintain an ideological position which supports secularism.

Secularization   A theory which argues that modernization brings a lessening of the role of religion in the public sphere and a subsequent decline of religious activity. The theory is contested on a number of levels, of which the following are most commonplace: i) it is only concerned with religious institutions and does not acknowledge that religion or spirituality may be flourishing in non-institutionalized forms; ii) it disregards the role of women in religion and privileges male religious behaviour; iii) it is Eurocentric in that it universalizes the situation of post-Enlightenment Western Europe to include all societies. (*See also* FUNDAMENTALISM; MODERNISM)

Seer   A term loosely applied but usually referring to a religious figure who has the ability to foretell the future. However, it is also used to describe a person who has achieved a high degree of wisdom through access to a divinity or special state of consciousness. (*See also* MYSTICISM; PROPHET)

Semantics   The study of meaning in language. Semantics can be both a branch of LOGIC and a branch of linguistics – in the latter it deals with the identification and ascription of meaning in human languages either across time or within a single period of time. Both are relevant for the study of religion, especially textual study where it is necessary to note how interpretation of religious languages such as Greek, Hebrew, Arabic and Sanskrit are utilized in religious arguments. (*See also* EXEGESIS; HERMENEUTICS)

Semiotics   The study of language as coded signs forming part of social, cultural or religious life. Language is interpreted in its widest sense as a means of communication consisting of symbolic codes – for example, codes of manners or religious RITES and ceremonies.

Shaman   A person who, because of his/her special personality and training, can make contact with the supernatural world. Through trance experiences he/she is able to contact the deity, spirits or world of the dead. Shamans maintain a special relationship with the worlds and beings that they visit, and can become possessed by supernatural beings when in trance states, facilitating communication between the worlds. Shamanic communication can be used to cure illness, to protect against hazardous enterprises such as hunting expeditions or long journeys, or to bless harvests. Usually shamanism is found in small-scale agricultural or hunting societies but has re-emerged as part of NEW AGE and NEO-PAGAN religions in advanced post-industrial societies. (*See also* EXPERIENCE; SEER)

Shrine   A SACRED location which marks a significant event in the life of a religion or may contain the body or RELICS pertaining to a person imbued with holiness. Shrine centres are deemed to be places where the barrier between the material and spiritual worlds is less and consequently contact with the divine is eased. As such, shrine centres function as amplifiers for the divine presence. Where shrines are located at the tombs of saintly persons, it is often believed that the remains or relics are endowed with holiness and can act as an intercessionary agent with the deity or are objects empowered with the ability to bless. Such blessings may offer rewards to the pious petitioner in this life or in an afterlife. Shrines are therefore important exchange centres and market places for SPIRITUAL CAPITAL. (*See also* EXCHANGE ACTIVITY; RITUAL).

Situationalism   Also known as circumstantialism, a position taken towards ethnicity that perceives it as responding to situations and dependent upon certain circumstances or interactions. Ethnic identity is regarded as a strategic decision in response to particular economic, social or political circumstances and when these factors change, ethnic identity is also transformed. (*See also* CONSTRUCTIVISM; ETHNICITY; PRIMORDIALISM)

Sociology of Religion   An academic discipline concerned with the questions pertaining to why religious beliefs and practices have been a central feature of human societies and cultures and why they have taken such diverse forms. Sociology of Religion is still highly influenced by the founding fathers of the discipline whose central stance was to dismiss religious beliefs and practices as irrational whilst at the same time observing and interpreting them through 'objective' and 'scientific' methods of study to determine their role in society. (*See also* REDUCTIONISM)

Soteriology   Originally a section of Christian theology that dealt with how SALVATION was negotiated for the Christian through the saving work of Christ in the world, the term is now more widely utilized to refer to all systems of salvation or liberation of the human spirit/soul/self existing in religious COSMOLOGIES.

Soul   Loosely used to convey an aspect of the human being that survives physical death and continues in some other kind of corporeal or incorporeal existence. Most of the world's THEISTIC religions, and the NON-THEISTIC Jainism, acknowledge some kind of soul entity, although circumscribed by the individual THEOSOPHY or COSMOLOGY held by each one.

Spiritual Capital   The tool for analysis of religious relations influenced by the language of economics. Spiritual capital assesses the accumulation of merit or non-material rewards that take place when EXCHANGE ACTIVITY occurs between followers of a religion and a divinity or other-worldly power. For example, in Hinduism worshippers may offer pieces of fruit, sugared crystals, or flowers to enshrined deities, and visitors to shrines may pay relatively large sums of money to purchase the objects required for offerings in order to receive the blessings or grace of the saint/deity. The rewards are intangible but form a kind of market place in which material goods are exchanged for spiritual rewards. However, spiritual capital creates actual micro-economies around PILGRIMAGE centres and other locations central to religious activity.

Spiritualism A complex of beliefs and practices concerned with contact with the spirits of the dead. Generally, the term is used to describe a number of Christian and non-Christian movements that have developed since the nineteenth century as a result of the activities of mediums who contact the dead though a variety of means. (*See also* EXORCISM; NECROMANCY)

Spirituality It is as difficult to define spirituality as it is to define religion but nevertheless the study of spirituality is rapidly developing into a sub-discipline of the study of religion. Most would agree that spirituality is something to do with inwardness, and this is interpreted in the traditional sense to signify an intense relationship with the SACRED involving deep emotive experiences of unity, joy, loss, gratitude and states of consciousness achieved through PRAYER, MEDITATION, reflection or remembrance. The study of religion will explore manifestations of inwardness in the major traditions – for example, Christian mystics, Hindu yogis and Sufis, but in contemporary Western societies, spirituality has also come to signify authenticity, and attempts to demonstrate commitment to truths that may be found outside of the realms of the sacred. As such, spirituality is shifting its territory to the domain of everyday life outside of religious structures and COSMOLOGIES. Finally, spirituality is being used consciously to create a distinct space from INSTITUTIONALIZED or organized religion. Paul Heelas (2005) defines this as 'subjective-life forms' of the sacred where forms of lifestyle are developing that assist people to live in accord with their own understandings of the sacred manifested within their individuality. (*See also* MYSTICISM; NEW AGE)

Structuralism An anthropological tool for the analysis of religion that is based on the premise that all human beings are thinking beings and create symbolic structures which are used in the manufacture of their social life. Thus, for example, the SACRED objects and MYTHS of religious life are representations of structures of the mind or symbolic bridges that carry thought back and forth between the real, the symbolic and the imaginary. For structuralists, the sacred only has existence where it appears in concrete social situations such as kinship, gender, marriage, providing legitimating authority. (*See also* ANTHROPOLOGY; FUNCTIONALISM)

Subaltern   Subaltern analysis begins from the premise that every powerful culture imposes its own IDEOLOGICAL and value-laden assumptions on the cultures of others, and so academic knowledge, in the words of Edward Said (1935–2003), is 'violated by a gross political fact'. Usually subaltern critiques of Western religious scholarship are maintained by scholars from parts of the world once under colonial domination and still feeling the impact of POST-COLONIALISM. Originating in the Indian subcontinent, subaltern perspective begins by displacing the central position of the European scholar as the subject of DISCOURSE with Indian society as the object and acknowledges that the indigenous scholar writes as a person shaped by the experience of colonial relations. Many subaltern scholars challenge the actual category of 'religion' as a Western construct. (*See also* COLONIALISM; ORIENTALISM)

Substantivist Definitions   Definitions of religion whose underlying assumption maintains that religion is a unique and special arena of human activity denoted by its relations with otherworldly beings or states of existence. Such definitions will usually refer to religion as having something to do with spiritual or supernatural worlds or entities. (*See also* FUNCTIONALIST DEFINITIONS)

Suffering   Most of the world's major religions, and a considerable number of the smaller, could be said to be systems that came into existence as a result of the existential crisis created by human misery and limitations resulting from temporal reality. One method of analysing a religion's constituent parts has been identified as questioning 'from what', 'by what' and 'to what'. Such an analysis would reveal some kind of identification of suffering and the ascription of a cause to the 'from what'. The 'by what' would provide a process through which something is eradicated. The 'to what' often ends that condition to be replaced by an eternal condition where suffering is terminated. (*See also* EVIL; REDEMPTION; SALVATION)

Supernatural   Simply the reality that lies beyond the natural world. The term 'supernatural' is sometimes preferred by scholars of religion to avoid definitions of religion that inevitably favour MONOTHE-ISTIC or THEISTIC traditions. Thus the problematic words like 'divinity', 'gods', 'God' or 'deities' can be avoided and replaced by a word that simply means 'above or beyond nature'. However, the word is laden with negative connotations arising from Christian use of the term, which usually refers to realms inhabited by ghosts and spirits, often associated with EVIL or dangerous powers.

Supramundane   *See* SUPERNATURAL.

Symbolics   A branch of theology which studies formal creeds and confessions of the various churches that constitute Christianity. Ecumenism has given a boost to this area of study in the twentieth century. (*See also* CREEDS; ECUMENISM)

Symbols   Religious symbols are the language that a religion uses, which have a value or meaning that pertains to the SACRED world and require interpretation by the believer. For example, a Christian needs the ability to interpret the world through the language of incarnation, resurrection, sin and SALVATION embodied in the story of Jesus and Israel. Such symbols bring meaning into human life and express the paradoxical nature of ultimate reality, they reveal something that is not perceived in everyday empirical reality and point to the sacred as a greater or deeper reality. (*See also* RITUAL; SACRED TEXTS)

Synchronic   The study of lived religions or more precisely the study of a religion looking at its present manifestations rather than its historical development. A synchronic approach is more likely to feature the beliefs and practices of all adherents, as opposed to focusing on elite groups or individuals, and may introduce the practice of fieldwork to the study of religion. (*See also* DIACHRONIC)

Syncretism   When narrowly defined, syncretism refers to the coming together of elements from two or more religions, resulting in the creation of an independent and new religious tradition. Thus it can argued that Sikhism came into existence as a syncretic mixing of elements from Hinduism and Islam. POST-COLONIAL studies of religion use the term in a slightly less prescriptive sense to explain the negotiation of multiple identities that arise from displacement, immigration and exile, where borders become less policed. In such cases, religious identities may creatively borrow and innovate without necessarily developing discrete new religions. (*See also* ECLECTICISM; HYBRIDITY)

Systematic Theology   The academic discipline which attempts to provide a rational account of the content of Christian DOCTRINE and ethical beliefs. It is usually studied alongside BIBLICAL STUDIES or church history and the combination of these subjects form the content of university Theology departments.

T

Taboo   A system of setting apart a person or an object as either SACRED or accursed, originating from a Polynesian word '*tabu/tapu*', meaning a restriction or prohibition related to the sacred. The term has passed into more general usage to describe ritual prohibition or the restriction on certain categories of people to enter the domain of the sacred. This may be temporary, as associated with periods of ritual impurity such as MENSTRUATION, or permanent, such as gender or caste restrictions.

Taxonomy   *See* CLASSIFICATION.

Teleological Argument   The philosophical arguments that assert that it is possible to move back from the observation of design in creation to posit the existence of an all-powerful and primal creator-god. (*See also* COSMOLOGICAL ARGUMENT; ONTOLOGICAL ARGUMENT; TELEOLOGY)

Teleology   The philosophical study of ends or final causes, especially the idea that the universe incorporates purpose and design. (*See also* TELEOLOGICAL ARGUMENT)

Textualist   A term used to describe a person or group which adheres strictly to the words of the text, often interpreting them in a very literal way. As such, textualism is very closely linked with religious FUNDAMENTALISM. The term 'textualist' has also been used as a label for a person whose knowledge of a religious text is very deep. From this definition, the term 'textualism' has been extended to include a scholar of religion whose focus is on interpreting and analysing SACRED TEXTS. (*See also* FOUNDATIONALISM)

Theism   A term used to denote a religious COSMOLOGY that acknowledges the existence and supremacy of a transcendent and personal God who creates, maintains and governs the world. Theism is closely connected with MONOTHEISM but extends into Indian and African traditions where one god amongst many may be given the attributes of the sole deity as in classical monotheism. (*See also* HENOTHEISM; POLYTHEISM)

Theocracy   A society which regulates itself through legal, social and political systems believed to come directly from a divine being. In such systems, rulers and power elites claim to govern with the authority derived from their status as representatives of the divine.

Theodicy   Historically a part of Christian theology which is concerned with the question of EVIL and its existence in the world. Classic theodicy has defended the omnipotence and goodness of God despite the presence of evil. However, it is sometimes used as an alternative term for NATURAL THEOLOGY. As with a number of terms used in Christian theology, its use has been extended to the study of other religions and the ways in which they reconcile the problem of the co-existence of evil and goodness with the existence of SACRED entities or states of consciousness considered to be ABSOLUTE.

Theology   Generally used to describe a number of disciplines which provide a rational account of the Christian faith, including BIBLICAL STUDIES, church history, SYSTEMATIC THEOLOGY, PASTORAL THEOLOGY and Christian ETHICS. The material covered and the approach used will depend largely as to whether the subject is studied in a secular institution of higher education or taught in a seminary or theological college. Considerable co-operation takes places between each mode of delivery.

Theonomy   An ethical position which understands moral life to be grounded in the ultimate authority of a divine being or divine will.

Theophany   A 'showing' or manifestation of a god or a divinity, either in a vision or in material form. (*See also* EPIPHANY; HIERO- PHANY; KRATOPHANY)

Theosophy   In a general sense, theosophy applies to any religious or philosophical system that claims an intuitive knowledge of the divine being, usually exhibiting aspects of PANTHEISM, MONISM or MYSTICISM. It is also the name for the esoteric movement begun by Madame H. P. Blavatsky and Colonel H. C. Olcott in New York in 1875 and moved to India in 1882. Drawing upon Eastern traditions and Western esotericism, including SPIRITUALISM, the Theosophical Society taught transmigration of souls, a universal brotherhood of humankind, along with complex esoteric understandings of the nature, origins and purpose of the universe and humanity. Theosophists were influential in the independence movements of India and Sri Lanka, and the movement massively impacted on the COSMOLOGIES of Western esoteric movements of the twentieth century.

Totem   A totem is an object which is imbued with sanctity resulting from its identification with a particular clan, tribe or people and from which all the members of that group are believed to be descen- dents. The totem functions as a guardian spirit and there are generally prescriptions on eating, killing or touching the totem animal. Some totems exist in the form of poles. (*See also* TOTEMISM)

Totemism   Beliefs and practices associated with religious forms that consider there to be a familial relationship between humans and nature. Totemism is a feature of some tribal societies where natural objects and creatures are seen to possess supernatural power. (*See also* TOTEM)

Traditions   A term used to describe religions which has common currency in the study of religion. Although more neutral than 'FAITH TRADITIONS' or 'BELIEF SYSTEMS', it rests on the notion that religions consist of a historical body of practices and beliefs that are passed down from generation to generation as a chain of memory. However, although many religions maintain this characteristic and even cement authority by conferring such traditions with divine origin, it has to be remembered that religions can come into existence as challenges to tradition. (*See also* CHARISMA; INSTITUTIONALIZATION)

Trance   An altered state of consciousness in which the religious specialist seeks to disconnect from conscious mental processes and connect to unconscious processes which are given free rein. Trance states are experiential and less concerned with conceptualization. Methods for attaining trance states include rhythmic and repetitive movements, breath control, chanting, attention absorption, relaxation techniques and the use of a variety of substances to enhance the capacity to switch away from the conscious self. Many religions possess techniques for inducing trance states in order to gain closer access to spirit worlds or the SACRED. (*See also* SHAMAN)

Transcendence   A concept of divinity that focuses on the idea of a supreme deity that is completely different from any other mode of being found in the created order and whose DOCTRINES essentially deal with the ways in which God's nature and form is completely different from that of men and women or other created beings. The concept of divine 'otherness' informs Judaic, Christian and Islamic doctrines and practice, although each religion maintains an understanding of IMMANENCE. The relationship between the two converges or diverges across religious history and between various strands of the respective faith. Eastern religions have been perceived as focusing more on the immanent. (*See also* MYSTICISM; NUMINOUS)

Truth-claims   Religions are concerned with the domain of the SACRED, a meeting of external and internal spaces set aside, imbued with special meaning and characteristics, to deal with ultimate concerns. Because religions have traditionally had a monopoly on the realm of the sacred, they have also provided METANARRATIVES, overarching ways of understanding creation and the purpose of human life that are regarded as truth. For thousands of years, the essential pursuit of knowledge was sought through the prism of religion. Religion was the repository of truth, originally embodied in

REVELATION or INSPIRATION and then developed through DOCTRINE and practice to sometimes become trans-global WORLD-VIEWS in which, for most adherents, the truths were non-negotiable. Contemporary Western society has given birth to rival truth-claims originating in scientific discovery, and today, increasingly, the study of religion has moved into the arena of social sciences and the humanities where religion is studied as human constructions of reality rather than divinely revealed and is perceived as cultural constructions rather than the domain of truth. Thus truth-claims remain contested between religions, but in addition, religions now defend their truth-claims against those maintained by the secular. (*See also* FOUNDATIONALISM; POSTMODERNISM; RELATIVISM)

U

Ubiquity The omnipresence of the ultimate being or the MONOTHE-ISTIC God. The ubiquitous nature of the THEISTIC deity has given rise to considerable speculation concerning how such a being can be everywhere without being physically located. The classic solution in Christianity has been to assert that God is present as the creative source of the existence of all things. Other theistic traditions see God's omnipresence in terms of timelessness or presence in eternity, but some Eastern forms of theism perceive the deity as literally present in matter, although not material. (*See also* IMMANENCE)

Universalism In Christianity, universalism is usually taken to be the view that ultimately all people will be saved, as a loving God would not condemn all to an eternal punishment. The position leads to the possibility that all the great religious teachers of the world's major faiths were inspired by variants of the same truth or the discovery of a perennial wisdom, consequently SALVATION is available to all without conversion from one religion to another. (*See also* ECUMENISM; INCLUSIVIST; PERENNIAL PHILOSOPHY; PLURALISM)

Utopian Most contemporary scholars of religion utilize the term to signify an ideal or longed-for existence or social system that does not exist or has not existed. Many religions posit a prior or future utopian condition, an alternative order free from the injustices or suffering of the present condition. Where such utopias are presented as actual historical or geographical locations, scholars are likely to be SCEPTICAL and to deconstruct religious constructions of reality.

Values   A recent term in ethics used to describe what a person holds as worthwhile, normative and occasionally prescriptive. The world's major religions can sometimes be depicted as 'value systems', as opposed to the conceptualization of ultimate reality. Religion is often perceived as the source of moral values and can set sanctions for obedience to them, justifying or rationalizing moral choices. However, religious values do not always reflect social values and can function as a critique of the prevailing value system. (*See also* ETHICS; TRUTH-CLAIMS)

Vernacular Religion   *See* APOTROPAIC.

Via Negativa   A theological position, often encountered in mystical traditions, which asserts that human language is hopelessly inadequate to describe either God or states of existence in which the ultimate reality is experienced as a form of union. Theologically the *via negativa* developed to counteract the possibility of ANTHROPO-MORPHISM in religious DISCOURSE concerning the nature of God. In mystical or contemplative traditions it has come to refer to methods that attempt to bring the practitioner to an awareness of 'nothing', in which the ultimate reality or God is discovered when everything else disappears. (*See also* MYSTICISM; VIA POSITIVA)

Via Positiva   A theological position that asserts that signs of a creator-God are discernable in the work of creation and in the doctrine of the human being made in God's image. In such thinking, either the wonder and order of creation or the highest human qualities are taken to be signs of God's perfection. In mystical or contemplative systems, the *via positiva* refers to methods that bring an individual into an awareness of God by focusing on something that reminds the practitioner of God's qualities or inspires feelings of appreciation and gratitude through such reminders. (*See also* VIA NEGATIVA)

Visions   Visions of the SACRED are claimed by individuals in many religious traditions. These can take the form of appearances of religious founders, divine beings such as angels or deities, sacred religious objects or texts. The vision of God in the MONOTHEISTIC traditions is more unusual, although it has a history in both Islam and Christianity. It is very rare that visions cross over into the religious symbolology of another tradition. For example, Christians do not normally have visions of Muhammad, or Buddhists visions of Jesus; however, there are some exceptions to this general rule. (*See also* MYSTICISM)

Voluntarism   Any theory which advocates the primacy of the divine will over the intellect or REASON. In Christian and Muslim theological debates these took the form of tensions between two viewpoints: i) things are good in themselves; ii) they are good only because God created them so. On the whole, Christian theologians wished both to maintain the freedom of God and to simultaneously protect the rationality of the moral and physical world. However, in Islam, the ORTHODOX position has been to assert that things are good only because God creates them so.

Witchcraft   Generally perceived to be a maleficent power innate in some people, usually women, to harm others psychically or by application of magic. In Africa, witches may not be conscious of their power but in European witchcraft this is rarely the case. Medieval Christianity was responsible for associating witchcraft with Satanic or EVIL powers, resulting in mass deaths of women throughout Europe before 1700. Witchcraft as a contemporary Western religion has attempted to remove negative connotations from witchcraft and assert its origins as a form of pre-Christian fertility religion that succeeded in surviving in spite of massive oppression. (*See also* PAGAN)

Womanist   A term used by black and Asian women to differentiate themselves from FEMINISM, which they critique as white and middle-class. The essential argument follows the line that black and other non-white women experience forms of oppression as a result of a complex interweaving of factors such as race, class and GENDER, and so cannot be simply reduced to PATRIARCHY.

Word of God   *See* LOGOS.

World Religion   A term which came into existence in the nineteenth century as part of the CLASSIFICATION of religions. Created to differentiate 'ethical' religions from nature religions or PRIMITIVE RELIGIONS that were located in tribes, 'world religions' referred to proselytizing religions which had expanded beyond the confines of a nation or a tribe to provide an overarching universalistic WORLD-VIEW.

World religions are those whose numbers or influence interact with and transform human history. Originally including Christianity, Islam and Buddhism, the list has been expanded to seven, incorporating Judaism, Hinduism, Taoism and Confucianism too. Other variations include Sikhism and Jainism. The classification is not without its critics who argue that it is ESSENTIALIST, NOMINALIST, and EVOLUTIONIST.

World-view   A concept common to most contemporary approaches to the study of religion. World-views are products of historical processes and can be defined as belief systems. In one of the best available definitions, W. Dilthey (1833–1911) stated that a world-view is 'one move from reality – it is not reality itself, but an interpretation of reality ... It is a total outlook compounded of EXPERIENCE, reflection, and interpretation ...' The world-view unites different levels of meaning and integrates different aspects of experience. Religions would only be one type of world-view in which truth is expressed within the context of divine or supernatural beings or worlds. World-views are often invisible, or taken for granted by those who hold them, and therefore part of the study of religion is to make them visible. (*See also* PHENOMENOLOGY OF RELIGION; RELATIVISM)